BACK ROOMS

Voices from the Illegal Abortion Era

ELLEN MESSER AND KATHRYN E. MAY, PSY.D.

A TOUCHSTONE BOOK
Published by Simon & Schuster Inc.
New York • London • Toronto • Sydney • Tokyo

Touchstone

Simon & Schuster Building
Rockefeller Center
1230 Avenue of the Americas
New York, New York 10020

Library of Congress Cataloging in Publication Data

Messer, Ellen.
Back rooms: voices from the illegal abortion era/Ellen Messer
and Kathryn E. May.
p. cm.
"A Touchstone book."
Bibliography: p.
1. Abortion—United States—Case studies. 2. Abortion—Moral and
ethical aspects—Case studies. I. May, Kathryn E. II. Title.
HQ767.5.U5M477   1989   89-6084
363.4'6—dc19   CIP

ISBN 0-671-68202-4 Pbk.

CONTENTS

ACKNOWLEDGMENTS

This book would not have been possible without the generous support of many people.

We are especially grateful to our diligent research assistant, Sandra Potter, for Sanding the Turnpike so we could get to the airport on time.

We thank Keith LaBudde for unfailingly stepping in to exorcise our computer gremlins.

Lilian Moore has been a mentor and guide throughout. She believed in us and the value of this project.

We appreciate Lawrence Lader, whose books so eloquently express his "one good idea." He was a fund of information in print and in person.

Thanks to Patricia Carroll, who helped to get this project underway.

And we want to thank our editor, Brian DeFiore, for his enthusiasm and his technical and creative skills, which helped to shape this book.

We express our deepest gratitude and admiration to the women and men whose voices form the substance of this book. Of course, without them, it could not have been written.

Finally, we acknowledge Studs Terkel for being a storyteller in the tradition that inspired us.

Ellen Messer wishes to thank the following people: Dick and Jake Phillips, who stood by me lovingly and spent many hours together freeing me to work. Margaret Rolnick for her valuable and enduring friendship. Mary Ann Mays, Harriet and Geoff Miller, Ralph and Adele Calcavecchio, Pam and Howie Bosworth, Helen Hosking, and Jane Allen, who helped me look beyond the moment. And I am grateful to all my friends and family who gave encouragement throughout the project.

Kathryn May wishes to thank the following people: Sam and Lilian Reavin and Laura Gardner, who adopted me and have provided the network and unfailing family support an author needs; my brother Tom, who knows how to laugh; and my children, who have taught me so much.

FOREWORD

Most of the readers of this book will be entering a world as strange and barbaric to them as historical novels in which an apprentice is hung by the neck until dead for stealing a loaf of bread. Although the props are familiar and the voices sound contemporary, although these women hold jobs as secretaries and businesswomen, marry and divorce, attend colleges familiar to us and travel to the same vacation spots, they live with a fear hard for us to understand. Only by comparison with the contemporary fear of AIDS can we hope to experience what the possibility of pregnancy meant to a woman when abortion was illegal. Then too desire or even true love might kill.

You are about to hear the voices of many women and a few men, who will describe to you a bizarre world. Remember that these traumatic circumstances are those in which you will soon be conducting your life, if the forces of reaction—who call themselves pro-life but value the lives of women not at all—are victorious in their attempt to deny women the right to choose.

It becomes evident to us as we read that Kathryn May and Ellen Messer are warm and gentle but probing interviewers who enable their subjects to speak in their own individual voices and to tell their stories with dignity and with feeling. There is an obvious quality of respect that shows both in how Messer and May approached their subjects and, more importantly, in the extent to which those interviewed felt safe in revealing some of the most painful experiences of their lives. In some cases, the woman interviewed had never told anyone exactly what had happened to her—not her husband or her lover, not her parents or her children.

We owe a debt of gratitude to all the women who speak to us honestly and often through tears of their experiences of forced motherhood, of signing their babies away, or abortions carried out without anesthetics. They share with us the fear that overcame them, the fear of bringing shame on their families, of losing their jobs and of ruining their relationships, of arrest and imprisonment, of accidental sterility, of infection and pain, of death. Even after death, they knew the shame would continue. Dying of an abortion was often covered up. Such a death would be a newspaper scandal if revealed, or else would be concealed if the family were able to persuade the doctor to fudge the cause of death.

We should remember too we are hearing only the voices of the survivors. The thousands of women who bled to death or died of septicemia or tetanus have left us no record of their agonies. Many of the women between these covers are college educated and had some resources. In that too they are unusual. The choices open to several of them, as unappetizing as they were, as dangerous as they were, represented opportunities simply not open to many women whose stories are not told here.

For instance, nowhere in this book will you read a story like my own, (the facts of which I incorporated in Jill's self-induced abortion in my novel *Braided Lives*). When I was eighteen, putting myself through college, poor and home for the summer to work a minimum wage job, I found myself pregnant. I was unable to locate a doctor or anyone willing to abort me. Determined to continue college, I did it myself, which almost cost me my life. The abortion in *Braided Lives* is as close to what I went through as I could manage to put down. I had no medical attention at any time. In the Detroit working-class neighborhood where I grew up, teenage pregnancy seems to me in retrospect as common as it is now, but I never knew anyone who had an abortion in a hospital, a doctor's office, or even from someone who posed as a doctor.

Often nowadays a young woman says to me that if the right to choose is repealed, her doctor will of course take care of her. This naive certainty comes from a lack of understanding of what illegality entails. The few doctors who did abortions safely, cleanly, and on a regular basis were protected by the local police, local governments, organized crime, or some combination. Those of us who did abortion referrals and helped women get abortions in those dangerous times remember such doctors fondly, but their very existence was due to corruption. If a "respectable" doctor agreed to perform an abortion, often he would not take any responsibility for consequences. If the woman hemorrhaged or became infected, running a fever, he would not respond.

There is an allusion in Lydia's testimony to an often forgotten trauma of that dreary time, one I remember best in the story of a friend of mine. Married for some years, she desperately wanted a child. Finally she succeeded in becoming pregnant. She was thin and frail. Even the early pregnancy was difficult for her, but she was delighted with her condition. Unfortunately, about halfway through her pregnancy, she began to miscarry. She was in pain and bleeding heavily. Under the law forbidding termination of pregnancy, she was guilty until proven innocent of having aborted herself. No painkillers, no assistance was given her when she went into the hospital, but rather she was treated as a suspected criminal, at a time when she was feeling close to suicidal over losing her baby. She was devastated psychologically, and that was essentially the end of her marriage.

It is unfortunate that most of the activists whose voices are heard are men. They are honorable men and deserve gratitude and recognition, but I have to say, in my time of working on circumventing and then repealing abortion laws, I met only women. It was women who created the underground networks of referrals and women who marched and shouted and fielded obscene phone calls and were bused to state capitols and to Washington to lobby and march again and again. It was women who made crude posters of other dead women and who lettered banners on sheets and who screamed themselves hoarse in the streets of cities and towns.

It is important to remember, whether you approve or disapprove of abortion, that other people will live their lives as best they can. Married women will make their decisions with regard to the needs of the children they already have, their husbands' desires and character, their families' economic status, and the other burdens on their time and energy. The legality or illegality of abortion is more of a determinant whether such a woman survives her choice than whether she makes it.

We certainly have an abundance of children born to single mothers now, with abortions legal and generally not prohibitively expensive, although a woman may have to travel a hundred miles or more to find a hospital or clinic that is willing to perform one. Fortunately, with the decay of the shame attached to bastardy and that word itself fading from the language except as a curse word with no more of its original content adhering to it than "damned" evokes theological connotations in "that damned cat," having a baby alone is a much sunnier possibility today than it was when the women between these covers considered their options. Of course, although society may not punish illegitimacy as once it did, the economic hardship and the lack of services a woman alone with a child experiences are trouble enough. Women alone with children lead the statistics we call the feminization of poverty.

However, whether abortion is legal or illegal, large numbers of women will resort to it, whether you are talking about women in a hunting and gathering society or women in highrises. Abortion is a necessary activity for our species, until and unless we can absolutely control our fertility, because we are bonded to our young for such a long time before they can carry out an independent existence. When we give birth, we are committing our time and our financial resources for at least the next eighteen years and perhaps longer. There are always going to be times when a woman can make such a commitment, and times when she cannot.

Sex leads to pregnancy less certainly than sugar leads to tooth decay, but we do not think of punishing teenagers for eating fast food by withholding dental work. We will not prevent women from terminating undesired pregnancies by making abortion illegal, dangerous, and not infrequently fatal. We will simply increase the amount of misery and danger in our society. Listen to these women tell you a portion of how it was for those who grew up in the nastiness of those times when abortion was a dirty and potentially lethal secret—and as common as the common cold.

MARGE PIERCY

INTRODUCTION

"I was talking with my niece and her friend—both of them are professionals in their mid-twenties—about the changes that have occurred for women in the past twenty years. I was describing how painful it was for me when I was nineteen and had to get married. They both looked at me as if I had two heads and said, 'Why didn't you get an abortion?' I said, 'Because it was illegal!' and they both just sort of stared at me. Then they said, 'Oh . . . yeah. . . .'"

It is hard to believe that it has been only fifteen years since we left behind an epoch when women agonized over what to do with an unwanted pregnancy. In its 1973 *Roe* v. *Wade* decision, the Supreme Court ensured reproductive choice for women by legalizing abortion. In the short time since then, we have developed a cultural amnesia so complete that young people appear to have no real knowledge about the shame and illegality which haunted the lives of their mothers and grandmothers for more than one hundred years in America.

This book is an oral history of those times. The stories included here are all true. It is not a controlled sociological study: We accepted the stories as they came, helter-skelter, by word of mouth, through a network of friends and acquaintances, through posted notices and author's queries. People heard of our project and came forward to offer their own remembrances and observations. All we asked was that they tell us their own story in their own words.

Initially, this was to be a collection of stories about the

women whose lives were dramatically and very directly affected by the fact that abortion was a criminal act: those who had illegal abortions and those who had to resort to a shotgun wedding, giving up a child for adoption, or raising an out-of-wedlock child. However, we were soon approached by others who broadened our thinking and our scope. Not only women responded; men also wanted to tell what it was like to be involved in an unwanted pregnancy. Medical people talked about their own moral convictions and expressed strong feelings of sympathy and outrage about the dilemma of women who needed their help so badly. Gradually, it became clear that many other voices had their place here.

Doing the interviews was profoundly moving. Many people had never told their stories before; few had ever told them in such intimate detail. As they talked, an initial hesitancy gave way to a flood of recollections, and then came the feelings. Voices faltered and faded, and many women wept.

Isolation was the common theme. Women couldn't turn to their mothers for help, even though they were desperate. Not one of them found out about an abortionist through her mother. There was no nurturing, no legacy of information from grandmother or mother to daughter. Instead they speak of estrangement from their families and society. Some told of feelings of alienation, others of loneliness and fear. Most had sealed up these memories years ago. One woman, who had told of grief and depression at each anniversary of her relinquished child's birth, called us to say, "It's been easier for me since I talked to you. The way you responded has helped to free me from those feelings of mourning. I hope other women can read this book and feel the same way."

As we went about gathering interviews, we had no difficulty finding women willing to talk about their illegal abortions. In fact, many sought us out. The women we found difficult to locate were those who had continued their unwanted pregnancies. The leads we did have to women who gave up a child for adoption, had a shotgun wedding, or raised an illegitimate child often ended with the women saying, "No, I cannot talk about this, even in confidence."

As the number of interviews grew, we found that during those years when abortion was a criminal act, there was a notable difference between the feelings of women who had had abortions and those who hadn't. There were women who felt they had to find a way to have an abortion because it seemed the only option that would allow them "to go on with life, even at the risk of losing it." They saw that choice as life-affirming. Afterward they felt relief—some even exhilaration—at the idea that they had been given a second chance. Not so for those who were unable to find their way to an abortionist and were forced to give birth to a child. For them, the ordeal was unfinished. Those who gave up a child for adoption have said that they feel a lifelong tie to a child who exists somewhere in the world, whose life goes on without them. They find themselves looking into the faces of children, searching, wondering if that child's life might someday cross theirs.

Those who raised a child out of wedlock faced social censure head-on. Nowadays, it barely raises eyebrows, but then it was an unforgivable transgression: a violation of the illusion of chastity. Obviously the woman had had sex without being married. The child was proof. She might hope to find anonymity as a new arrival in a different town, by creating the deception that she was widowed or divorced. If she were unsuccessful, her child would be branded with the stigma of having been born a bastard.

Then there were shotgun weddings, which came in two kinds. There were those couples who would have gotten married anyway, who rushed the nuptials, with a baby on the way, and made the best of it. There were others who never intended to marry, but did what they thought they had to do. Even though more than two decades have passed since her unplanned marriage, one woman told us, "I saved face at the cost of giving up my autonomy, and the price I paid was years of my life . . . I still feel anger and resentment about that."

In 1973, the Supreme Court voted 7–2 in favor of the decision that legalized abortion. Since this decision, fervent right-wing anti-abortionists have mobilized a well-organized, highly vocal force to attack the law. There has been little danger that the people of this country would agree to changing the abortion laws through an act of Congress. An abortion amendment would be unlikely, since poll after poll has shown that Americans overwhelmingly favor free choice in matters of reproduction and family planning. The danger exists on another flank.

The "Right-to-Life" movement has been unrelenting in its effort to influence the executive and judicial branches of government, and to exert pressure on the Supreme Court to overturn the law. As a result of this pressure, the Supreme Court agreed to hear a series of cases on the issues. On June 11, 1986, a seriously divided Court affirmed the law by a margin of 5–4. Each time a case involving abortion is heard by the Supreme Court, there is a danger that the *Roe* v. *Wade* decision could be reviewed and overturned.

Through the testimony offered here, we hope to fortify and strengthen those who believe that freedom for women is essential to us all. The men and women we interviewed entrusted us with information they hoped we could use to help those who come after. They fear that what happened in the past could happen again and they want to prevent it. In one woman's words, "It was a very desperate time. I think people forget. . . . We took incredible risks. Young women think that if it became illegal it would just be a legal question. Well, when it becomes illegal, the places to have abortions done will go away, and again it will become a furtive, subterranean thing to get an abortion; ask the guy who steals cars, he'll know where you can go.

"When I see everything that's happening today, and the threat of losing our rights, I remember what the options were and just find that unthinkable, like going back to witchburning."

KATHRYN E. MAY
ELLEN MESSER
High Falls, New York
1988

Since the first edition of this book, we have added an interview with Patricia Maginnis, a founding member of the National Abortion Rights Action League. Her extraordinary contributions to the abortion rights movement epitomize the pioneering effort of a generation of courageous women.

KATHRYN E. MAY
ELLEN MESSER
1989

"No woman can call herself free who does not own and control her body. No woman can call herself free until she can choose consciously whether she will or will not be a mother."

—*Margaret Sanger*

BACK ALLEYS, DARK STREETS

Caroline

"I was raised as a good Catholic girl in a good Catholic family, and abortion was not a thing I was even very comfortable thinking about."

When Caroline first heard about plans to write this book, she wanted very much to be involved and tell her story. "I want other women to know how terrible an illegal abortion can be." However, she arrived half an hour late for the interview, saying, "I'm usually very punctual, but these memories are difficult to talk about, and I think I was trying to block them out."

Caroline is a forty-four-year-old woman who is a librarian at a college in a small rural Massachusetts town. As she talks about why she chose to have an abortion and recalls the pain of the experience, she is frequently overcome with tears.

I really don't know exactly where to begin. When I start thinking about it one thing leads to another. One of the things that occurs to me now as I think about it is how interesting it was that I really totally forgot that I was planning to come talk to you this evening, because there is a part of me that tried to block out this experience for a long time. . . . For a long time I think I drank to avoid the feelings. And it wasn't until quite recently, five years ago, after I had stopped drinking for a while, that I went through a whole period of really reliving the terror of this experience. I think that I just effectively pushed it back.

At any rate, when it happened I knew right away that I was pregnant. It was in the summer, between my junior and senior year of college. I was going to college in Cleveland, living there for the summer. And somehow I just knew. I remember walking over to the Cleveland Museum of Art the very next day, to the park around the lagoon, and sitting with the young artist involved. I said that I thought I was pregnant, that I had a sense I was pregnant.

It was the first and only time that I was ever sexually intimate with this man. He was a young artist whom I had been seeing for some time. I wasn't particularly physically attracted to him, but he had always pressed. I liked him and we had gone out for some time. On this particular occasion we went ballroom dancing. I can't remember where, but we drove some distance with another couple to a big ballroom where there was an old-time band. We had dinner at their house first, and then went dancing and had a lot to drink. And when we came back from that evening he was pressing me and pressing me and pressing me, and I just finally got to the point where I couldn't struggle with it anymore. So I gave in. It certainly was not a planned sexual encounter. At the time I hadn't done anything about birth control for myself and somehow I immediately had the sense that I was pregnant, which did turn out to be true.

I really didn't know what to do. I knew, though, that having a baby would ruin my whole life. The man involved felt responsible and wanted to marry me, and he attempted to persuade me once I knew I was pregnant. I didn't want to marry him—I thought it was a very weak reason for getting married. He offered me a ring. He had just taken a teaching job and he wanted me to come and live with him in Columbus and have the baby. But I did not want to do that. I really did not know what to do. I spent a lot of time just seeing my life in a shambles. I thought about going to a home for unwed mothers and I thought about how my family would deal with it, how it would affect my college career, my scholarships, my job. How could I go away and then come back and pick up the pieces. . . . I don't know when I really started to think about an abortion. First, I thought about marriage and rejected it as an option. Then I envisioned the whole business of going away to a home. I couldn't even imagine telling my parents. I had lots of younger siblings at home and I couldn't imagine being at home pregnant. It was just unthinkable. At any rate, once I decided that I just really couldn't put my family through the shame, didn't want to put myself through whatever happens in those Booth homes for unmarried young ladies, and totally rejected marriage, I started thinking that I would try and find a way of having an abortion.

I had earlier helped a friend get an abortion. It had seemed to be a fairly easy thing to do. She was the daughter of a doctor, and she had had a previous abortion in Chicago. In this case she was pregnant and just not facing the reality of that. Finally I became very concerned about her, concerned that it would be too late, and took it upon myself to call her father, arrange to meet with him, and let him know that his daughter was pregnant. After really thinking through the implications, I decided that I had to risk her never speaking to me again, that her life was really in the balance. It was simple once her father knew. Very shortly she was in the hospital. . . . A week later she was back in school looking fine, feeling fine, and that was the end of it. It was easy for her because she had the right connections. It wasn't so easy for me.

Things at that time in Cleveland were very tight. There had been several incidents reported in the paper. An abortion ring had been broken up. It was 1963, and when I followed up on the few leads there were, it seemed that it was absolutely the worst possible time in about five years to have an abortion in Cleveland. The police were following up on everything, and it was literally impossible. I knew of someone who had managed to arrange an abortion, I think in Pennsylvania, for a thousand dollars. I didn't have a thousand dollars.

In the meantime the weeks were going by and I was more

pregnant all the time and it was really getting to the point that if I didn't do something soon it was going to be too late. As I think back about it, what's incredible to me is that I never thought of going to my friend's father. I may have, but I can't recall whether I thought about and rejected it. As I'm talking to you, I'm really struck that I didn't try to contact my friend's father, but for whatever reason, I didn't. I was greatly confused about taking that step, to have the abortion. And being raised as a good Catholic girl, it was not a thing that I was even very comfortable thinking about. But I didn't feel that I had any other option. I was getting pretty desperate by this time because I was nine weeks pregnant. I finally located an abortionist in Youngstown, Ohio. It was going to cost one hundred dollars. I contacted the artist in Columbus, who was very angry that I was taking this step and told me he was not going to participate in it. But, with great reluctance, he gave me the money.

I don't know what happened to the people who had been my friends. I really isolated myself in this. I had not talked to them. For some reason the women who were my friends had not been involved. It must have had something to do with the fact that I judged myself very harshly because I was pregnant and because I didn't want to bear the child. I did confide in a social worker I made friends with during this crisis. I also became friendly with a younger couple, and the four of us together made this little trip to Youngstown, Ohio, about an hour and a half away, to get my abortion. I think at this point I was twelve weeks pregnant. It was very late.

This so-called doctor—this man who called himself a doctor—had two businesses. He was a bookie and he was an abortionist. He was an elderly man in a ramshackle little house in a disreputable, shabby section of Youngstown. It in no way fit my image of a doctor's house and office. I had never seen a doctor who lived like this man or looked like this man, or acted like this man. I don't recall seeing any medical certificates on his walls. I don't think anyone who was a doctor would also be a bookie. I think there was some actual gambling going on while we were waiting. But that was my only option, and I was very desperate to go through with it. I recall questioning whether he was a doctor at all. I also questioned what I was getting myself into, and whether I was going to survive this.

He had a room with a chair and stirrups set up. I went in and it was all very, very secretive. The money had to be in cash, in certain denominations, and it had to be given to him in an envelope. He checked it very thoroughly to make sure it wasn't marked. He was very concerned about keeping the cops out of his operation. But I took the risk of turning my life over to him because I didn't think I had another choice.

The social worker came with me and the other couple waited at the motel. The "doctor" also insisted that you had to be married. His scruples were such that he would only do this for married women. I think I borrowed a ring to wear and pretended to be married to the social worker. I remember his questioning us about it and giving me a hard time. I was just terrified. But then he said, "Oh, whatever," and took me in. He explained he was doing a saline injection and that there should be some cramping and the abortion would happen within twenty-four hours. After he finished, we left and went back to the motel. We all waited, and waited and waited and waited through the night and nothing happened. So we all drove back to Cleveland.

I don't know how many days passed; I did a lot to block out this experience. But I do know that when I finally aborted I was alone in my room in the dormitory at school. I went through at least twelve hours of labor alone in my room.

It was more terrible than I ever imagined, partly because I was alone, partly because I was scared. I was timing the contractions and I just didn't think I could bear anymore. I didn't feel I could cry out for help, and I just remember thinking, "I'm going to get through this." I know that it went on for at least twelve hours. I remember noticing that the contractions were getting more frequent and more frequent, five minutes, then four minutes, then three minutes, and then there was a lot of blood and there was a fetus. I was really beside myself, and terrified. I didn't know what to do. There was more blood than I ever imagined. I used one of these metal waste baskets we had in the dorm rooms and I remember it being filled up. I think I had gone through a whole night and it was now midmorning, and there weren't many people around. I managed to get to the bathroom, very surreptitiously. I was terrified of someone discovering me, of being arrested.

I remember taking this fetus and not knowing what else to do but flush it down the toilet. And I was terrified that it wasn't going to go down, and that it would clog up the system, that somehow, some way I would be found out. The whole system would be clogged up. They'd have to call a plumber and then there would be this hunt to find out who did this terrible thing in the dorm, and I'd be tracked down and prosecuted. I was really in shock and just terrified.

I had managed to get through that night and morning, by sheer grit and determination. I'm very stubborn. Somehow I thought then it would be over, but it wasn't over. It went on and on. I kept hemorrhaging and it just wouldn't stop. It went on for days and days and I didn't know what to do. I was afraid to say anything to anyone. I really didn't think of going to a doctor; I didn't think of going to a hospital. I was afraid I was going to be arrested and prosecuted. And I just kept hoping it would stop. It was getting close to Thanksgiving, and I continued to bleed. I tried to go on with my life, which consisted of going to school and working.

I had become pregnant in August, and the abortion was in early November. I remember going home for Thanksgiving and wondering whether I'd have the strength to take the bus. While I was home my mother kept saying, "I think you're anemic." And I remember being very drained and wiped out.

Early in December, I became friendly with a very gentle, brilliant but quite crazy college student who had been hospitalized when he was suicidal. I remember going to a fraternity Christmas dance with him, getting all dressed up and going to the beauty shop to get my hair done, which is what you did in those days when you went to a fancy college formal dance. I was hardly able to walk home from the beauty shop to the dormitory. But I was going on; I was not going to let this get me down. I went to the dance that night so weak that I couldn't dance. The boy was a very kind and gentle person who had problems himself. That night I found myself confiding in him that I couldn't dance because I was so weak. I'd had this abortion, and I was still bleeding and I didn't know what was wrong. He said he would see what he could do.

He came to see me the very next afternoon. He'd gone to church and afterward talked to the rector of the Episcopal Church in Shaker Heights, because he didn't know what else to do or who to talk to. And the rector, to whom I shall be forever grateful, was very wise and humane and kind. He asked my friend to bring me to him.

I remember being driven to, of all places, this Gothic edifice, and going into a formal book-lined study. The rector, a gentle Christian man, expressed a lot of sympathy for me. When I told him what had happened, he was very angry. He remarked that he had lots of parishioners who had money to fly to Sweden to get an abortion, and it was really criminal that just because I didn't have money I'd had to go through this kind of experience. He thought I clearly needed medical attention and he was going to do something about it. Now, I was terrified of this, because I didn't want my parents to find out and I didn't want to be arrested. So he reassured me, and he called one of the doctors in his congregation and made an appointment for me that very afternoon.

I think my friend drove me there and left me. When I finally saw the doctor, I got really frightened. He was so appalled at my condition that he said, "Do you realize you could have killed yourself?" He immediately called and made arrangements to get me admitted to the hospital. He said they would have to do some transfusions because I had lost so much blood, and asked me if I knew of anyone who could give blood. I called my friend and asked him if his fraternity would be on notice to contribute some blood.

At the doctor's insistence I took a cab back to the dormitory.

My friend met me there and drove me to the hospital. They gave me about five pints of blood. After they built me up they did a D&C. I wasn't yet twenty-one, so they couldn't do it without my parents' permission. The doctor called and spoke to my mother and said that I had been having some menstrual problems, and there was nothing to be concerned about; the D&C was just a routine procedure and would help. He said that I was quite anemic. My mother gave her permission and never knew that I'd had an abortion. She said to me afterward that she always thought I was anemic.

I must have been in the hospital five days. The Episcopal Church paid my hospital bill and the doctor never charged. I was very thankful, and totally done in at the end of that ordeal.

I didn't feel guilty. I was determined once I made the decision to follow through with it, and I did.

I really was desperate. If I had not been so desperate I wouldn't have opted for the Youngstown, Ohio, connection. I certainly wouldn't want anyone to have to live through the experience that I lived through. There's no need for it. I did make choices: I considered and chose not to choose marriage. I chose not to be an unwed mother. Abortion was the option of last resort, but I chose it because it seemed the only option that would allow me to go on with my life, even at the risk of losing it.

Kathleen

Kathleen is an editor and journalist working for a large metropolitan newspaper.

I had an illegal abortion in 1969, in Missouri, where I was going to school.

I was caught in a triple whammy of growing up Catholic, suddenly finding my sexuality, and not having birth control as an option. And then suddenly I found myself pregnant. It was at that point that I had to do a lot of hard thinking. I had watched other people make the decision—not a lot, there wasn't a lot of talking about sexuality at that time in rural Missouri—and then when it happened to me of course I felt trapped and I didn't have a lot of time. The counseling available would tell you to go to a home and have the baby and give it up for adoption.

I was in my senior year of college. I had worked my way through, and I was in no position to give it all up. Marriage was an option, but I was desperate not to do that, not to fall into that trap. So I went to my most liberated friend, and we put an ear to the ground and we found out about this abortionist who I went to, full knowing that I was risking my life.

It was a filthy operation. It was a rural town, a residential house, and it looked like a flophouse where this M.D. kept an office just for this purpose. The office itself was filthy, he smelled of booze, and we had a very awkward time because of course I was fidgety and nervous, and sort of numb.

When it was over, he tried to kiss me, which didn't seem so untoward. I mean, the whole thing was so tacky and tawdry and filthy that it didn't seem to me all that unusual that a person of his caliber would also try to do that.

It cost, I think, three hundred dollars, which was a lot of money for me at that time. And it didn't end there. That weekend I was to stay at the house of an acquaintance that we had found whose girlfriend was also having an abortion. So the two of us—it turned out to be three of us who had all used this same person—stayed in an apartment, of course not knowing what was going to happen to us. We were there for probably two days. One of the women, a very young girl of about sixteen or seventeen, became very ill and eventually had to be taken to a hospital. All we knew at that moment was that she was being hauled off to some uncertain fate, but later we found out she developed all kinds of infections and complications. The other woman was experiencing some difficulty, but not too much.

Fear was probably the hardest part. I was having no physical problems. At first I thought I had just been lucky, but it turned out several weeks later that I was still pregnant.

My boyfriend of four years was living in St. Louis, which was the nearest major city, and he began to ply the uncertain network of illegal doings in St. Louis, where you could have it done for one thousand dollars.

He, like myself, had been brought up a Catholic and his idea was, well, you get married and you have the child and you go on living and you make the best of it. I have to give him credit. He backed up my decision, found this option, and we borrowed the money.

This other operation was a little more professional. It's hard to think of it in terms of today, but it was a walk-up apartment that looked like it had formerly been a beauty parlor; little gilt chairs and mirrors, and an old woman who took care of "the women." I forget why, but I was there a day early and stayed with the old woman. The next day a very professional-looking woman doctor came, and no chitchat about what she was going to do. She used the vacuum procedure, and . . . cash on the line.

The second abortion was successful, and I had no other health ramifications from that, although later that spring I was hospitalized for a mysterious ailment which today I have figured out was colitis. I remember going through a battery of tests in a religious hospital in St. Louis, and the doctor kept asking, "Has anything happened in your life to make you so anxious?" and luckily I was in my senior year and everything was anxious. But the whole experience left me so . . . it's a wonder I didn't have a nervous breakdown.

Probably the only thing that gave me the strength to have the abortion was that I felt that I would just as soon die as be trapped into poverty and motherhood, and that's what it would have been. I didn't think it would have been a fair life for a child or a mother. I would have fallen into a loveless marriage of one sort of another, and I would be divorced today, and I would probably have had an unhappy kid.

I knew that I had been playing Russian roulette with sex for over a year, but, you know there wasn't a lot of thinking about anything, about your sexuality. There certainly wasn't any of the discussion that women would have today about what to do or how to prevent pregnancy, if you ever thought about it. Sex was something you did furtively. Even if you were going with somebody, as I was, it wasn't assumed that you were having a sexual relationship. You had to do it "under wraps," so to speak, and then you became pregnant. When I think back on it, it was inevitable. It's amazing that it didn't happen sooner, but at that time I thought it was damned unlucky.

It was a heavy decision to make. I was already separating from my religion, but it was not just a decision about what to do with your body; you were deciding your eternal fate, and I had to decide whether I believed in all that stuff. And that was the kind of thinking I had always deferred. You kind of move away from your religion, and one day something happens and you wake up and say, "I don't believe that anymore." I wasn't ready for that, but I had to make a decision. I had read what the Church said about the beginning of life and eternal damnation and excommunication and all that stuff. And that's what it was: excommunication, automatic. You know, between you and God.

So I sort of decided that I needed control over my life now, and, you know, wasn't going to hedge my bets against an uncertain eternity at that point. I feel that in a very basic way, at the last minute, I found a way to take control of my life, and it's paid off.

I was twenty-one, but I was a very naive twenty-one. I hadn't given full thought to my sexuality because I'd spent a lifetime not thinking about it, and that was true of a lot of women. It made it very difficult to decide what your values were, because you had your values, and what you really *did*.

In Missouri, we were probably behind other areas of the country. We were still waiting to be drafted into the sexual revolution. I think it was considered the "just deserts" of sex before marriage that you would have to be in such a predicament. Women dropped out of school to go to these little houses for unwed mothers, with uncertain futures, and the stigma that was attached was incredible. The hypocrisy was amazing.

There were sororities on campus. That was sort of like the Good Housekeeping Seal of Approval—if you were a sorority girl. They used to have something called an ethics council or something. It was like a morality council that would decide . . .

One sorority sister went out with a very loose-lipped fraternity man, and apparently they were having sexual relations, and he went around talking about it all over the place. He talked about it to the fraternity that corresponded with my sorority, and so the morality board got together. I remember we were all called together for a meeting, and she was hauled up in front and told that she was bringing a bad reputation to the sorority by having sexual relations. And I remember I was horrified by that meeting, but I wasn't about to speak out because that would mean that I thought it was okay that she was having sexual relations.

They ruined this girl. She eventually had to leave the sorority because she was so alienated from the other women. And why? Because she was doing anything different? No! Because she was doing it with the wrong guy! But anyway, the beauty of it was that the woman who headed that council had to get married at the end of that year. And then it was bridal showers and confetti.

But what about all the others who had to get married? Every year it was somebody, and actually as the years went on more and more of those women on that original morality council did get into dilemmas like that: married to some guy they dated twice! To me it was a big awakening about women and the way we treated each other.

This whole anti-abortion thing, that they could make it a question of morality . . . I just can't bear to think that that could happen again.

Lila

We talk in Lila's hotel room. Although she arrived only yesterday, she has already converted the room into a working office. Everything is in its place. Lila is a successful businesswoman and has recently earned a doctoral degree. She has the air of a woman who is sure of herself and knows what she wants.

I had been dating Joseph almost a year, yes, I'd met him in the spring of my freshman year and I was still dating him in the fall. He was an African graduate student in engineering. He was very much attached to me and I was fond of him. I think he liked me as an individual and he also liked me ritualistically. He liked what I stood for, he loved my family, and he was very close to my mother. He had been home for Easter holidays with us. He was a Catholic also, and Black Catholics were really hard to find. The fact that he was foreign kind of threw my parents off because they didn't want me moving off to Africa if this thing went any further, but he was as much involved with my family as he was with me. And that's kind of, I guess, important to the story.

During this time going to Planned Parenthood was not something you did unless you were married. And I was a Catholic girl from Des Moines, Iowa, so I didn't know from going to Planned Parenthood. I did find out later that some of the women who came to the college had come with diaphragms, which I thought was totally, incredibly avant-garde, mature, and hip, because I didn't know much about diaphragms. It was the classic morality of the fifties and sixties. You were allowed to sleep with somebody as long as you only slept with one person at a time and as long as you were in a steady relationship. A person would be looked down on if she slept with several people or slept around. It wasn't cool to sleep with someone who everybody knew was seeing somebody else, for example. As long as you did it like a married couple but just weren't married yet—as long as you were a real couple. I mean you didn't go around blabbing about it but it was all right. The only contraception that I knew about from high school days was condoms and the rhythm method. When I was sixteen I started being sexually active, but only infrequently. It was part of the culture that you weren't supposed to seem too ready or willing. You were always supposed to go through several sessions of fighting the guy off. I mean even if it was your steady boyfriend there was lots of heavy petting and once in a while things could go all the way. Also there were very few opportunities, and I wasn't one for doing things in the back seat of a car. So my boyfriends always were guys who were a little older, and more established than one would expect people to be at that age. They had an apartment for example, so that they could set up housekeeping and play house and have a "relationship." So anyway, the contraception that I used when I was in Des Moines was usually the rhythm method, because since I wasn't having sex every time I dated the guy, I could fight him off, being coy and whatnot when I knew it wasn't okay, and then I could "go over" when I knew it was just three days after my period stopped. And it worked. I never told the guy this. I knew what I was doing.

Now I'm a college student and I'm seeing the culture where, when women have steady relationships with fellows, they go and stay with their fellows every weekend. This was not the same culture as the late sixties and seventies, this was kind of different. This was maybe marriage. I don't know what the hell you called it. And it was considered very prestigious to put out a sign on your door that you were away for the weekend and could be reached at so-and-so's place, because it meant you had a steady relationship. You weren't sitting in your room at the dorm studying, and you weren't at some beer blast at the frat, and you weren't, God forbid, sleeping around. You were mature, you were grown-up, you were above that. You had your relationship, and now you could focus on your studies. You got permission from your parents for unlimited overnights. You kind of talked them into it—they didn't know why. They couldn't figure out these forms. "Just sign here." So they gave you unlimited overnights so then you could be prestigious. But of course this played total havoc with the rhythm method. Neither Joseph nor I had too much of an idea of other than textbook things of what to do about contraception, so he used condoms. I also used foam. I heard about it through discussions in the dorm and you could buy it in the drugstore. We were very middle-class 1950s: everything was planned. There was no spontaneous sex. You had sex at night in bed. But on one occasion, in the fall, one of Joseph's apartment mates was away. He had a huge beautiful bedroom which had a beautiful view of the river. He also had the biggest bed. He was a swinger. He was an African too, but he was from another African country, and that's how everybody explained why David was such a swinger. He capitalized on his handsome foreignness. He had the bachelor swinging pad with this huge bed and a mirror overhead.

Joseph and I had gone to dinner (I wish I could say we were drinking, but we hadn't been). We were kidding around and we went to David's room, and we started fooling around and fell into bed. We fell into his bed and had sex, and my period did not come the next time. I must have told my friend right off because now starts this really very poignant story. I was determined not to have the baby, but Joseph told me that it was my choice because he was ready to get married. He meant it; I was playing at it. Not playing with him, but I realized when I got pregnant I was playing at it. This is what you were supposed to do. I liked the guy, but when he started talking about marriage and babies and stuff I wasn't ready. I wanted to finish my education. I didn't want to be married when I got out of college. I didn't want to be a married student with a baby trying to finish up college for two years. I really couldn't imagine having a baby by this guy. I think I didn't want to go back to Africa to stay. I really didn't want to resolve the cultural conflicts with him. I think there was a lot of cultural prejudice as to why I didn't want an African kid. I didn't rationalize this—I heard it was really awful for Black women who went to Africa as wives. The African women hated them, and the African men all thought they were whores and chased after them when their husbands weren't home.

Joseph and I were very close. He was very paternal toward me anyway, because of culture and age, and now he was worrying me more than I was worrying myself. I was just trying to take care of business. He was on the phone every three hours, every day, every night. What did he used to call me, what was his nickname? His nickname for me was "Mommy," even before I got pregnant. The way he used to say it was "Mummy"—he had a British accent—"How are we doing?" Now coming out of his culture, to be a mother is a very high compliment. He already perceived me as maternal, and then he met my mother, who was the classic mommy. She starched underwear, she cooked everything from scratch, she never wore pants a day in her life. He would get on the phone and I would be so hassled because I was just trying to deal with business, and I would have to deal with his emotionalism. "Has anything happened yet?"

What I first did out of my own naiveté was to ask people in the dorm, friends, "What can I do?" I only remember one remedy—it has a memory for me to this day—very hot baths and gin. To this day I can't stand the smell of gin. I must have tried that about three or four nights. It didn't work.

I decided to ask my stepmother in Des Moines if she could help me. Now, my stepmother's a real meddling and involved lady—she knows everything about everybody every place. She's still like that to this day. She's wonderful and horrible all at the same time. Anything you tell her that you need, she will get it. She knows how to do it. She is a manipulative, powerful, resource-building person. So I got her on the phone, not my mother. My mother had ambivalent feelings about women getting educated anyway, and she didn't quite know why my sister and I were going off and getting all this higher education. She would have been angry and she probably would have put great pressure on me to get married and have the kid. So she never knew anything about any of it. My mother is dead now, and to this day the fact that my stepmother knew and mother didn't gives me great remorse and grief.

So, I told my stepmother I was pregnant and that I didn't want to have the baby, I wanted to finish school, and she says, "Fine, I'll call you back." In two hours she called me back. She said, "Come to Des Moines this weekend." I said, "How much will it be?" and I think she said one hundred dollars. I felt nothing. I didn't feel anxious. I think I was stupid. No, I was not stupid, I think there's a part of me, either it's a survival mechanism or a character defect—really, I'm serious. When I hear of what other people went through . . . I just went to take care of business. To say I was numb gives me more credit for being thrown out of joint by this thing. I think I was overcontrolled. I just got on the train. Not only did I not think about the moral or ethical implications, I didn't think about the physical possibilities. Maybe I didn't know. Maybe I knew and just blocked it out. But I said, "I'm going to go have this thing and I'll be back to school on Monday."

We must have done it on a Friday night. I think she picked me up from the train station. We went to the poor section of town. I remember not seeing anyone—just looking straight ahead—that there were shadows to the side, and because it was still warm, there were people sitting out on the stoops and out on the steps. Now, I'm the daughter of a well-known man in our town, not to mention my stepmother. Whenever I saw these townspeople I saw them as my father's daughter. They were renters of his apartments and frequenters of his pool hall. I was seen as so-and-so's daughter. So now that I'm going to this house where everybody knows there's an abortionist that has an apartment in the back, I was even more self-conscious. And my stepmother greeted everybody and she just walked me through the door. Because everybody knows her, they just said hi, nobody questioned, nobody said anything. But I think everybody knew. Why else would we be down there? She'd made preparations, she'd probably talked about it. It was in a first-floor flat, one of these frame houses that was broken up into apartments.

It was a kitchen table, coat hanger abortion. It took maybe six minutes. I got on the kitchen table. I think my stepmother gave me a drink of brandy or something, and she said, "Now this may hurt a little bit." She held my hand and this woman stuck a piece of coat hanger into my vagina. She stuck the coat hanger in, a piece that had been sterilized or whatever the hell she had done, and then my stepmother said, "Okay, now you get dressed." And what you were supposed to do was leave that in there until you started to abort. And then I left. I remember walking out with this coat hanger between my legs. I went back home to my father's house.

That evening I started bleeding and I think I was feeling cramps. Yes, I remember I had cramps, and my stepmother said, "Go to bed," and she put me to bed. I remember her giving me a drink, and giving me aspirin and I went to sleep and to me it was fine, because it was better than I would do with my menstrual cramps. I got up very early in the morning and went to the bathroom and there was just this passage of blood and a clot that was slightly bigger than the clots I usually passed during my menstrual period. I realized that that was the fetus passing, that what I had taken as another blood clot was actually the abortion. I felt a little mixed then because it seemed like I should have done something at that moment. The next month my period came on time.

The only trouble I have with it is somehow thinking I should have been more concerned. If for no other reason than for the physical reality. I could have died. I could have become sterile.

All this terrible stuff could have happened. The more I think about it now, the more horrible I realize it was. When I read about people on the kitchen table I say, "I had one of those." But I was so blanked out, I didn't know what the hell I was doing.

Back at school, I went to Planned Parenthood. First I went to Woolworth's and bought a wedding ring for two dollars. I remember I told my friend, "This is what I'm going to do, I think I'm going to get on the pill." Even though we didn't know what the pill meant at that point. So I bought the wedding ring in Woolworth's and went on down to Planned Parenthood and put my boyfriend's name down as my husband and put his address down as mine, and I got a diaphragm.

I think it was rarer for Black women to have chosen to have an abortion back in the bad old days. One reason people cite is that having a child enhanced a Black woman's self-esteem. And they still like to talk about that stuff. I would suggest that another reason is because many Black women didn't know where to find one. I happened to be in one of the so-called prestigious Black families in my hometown, so I knew how. If it was difficult for a white woman to find one, it was impossible for a Black woman to find one, especially a poor Black woman. I had friends back in Des Moines who had babies at twelve, fourteen, sixteen; some of them are grandparents now. People did things like try to drink gin. By the time they'd tried all of those wives' tales, they'd gotten to the third or fourth month. Even if they found somebody, by that time none of the kitchen table abortionists would touch them.

I was dating somebody who could hand me one hundred dollars. Many poor Black women were not in a relationship with a man who could have afforded that. So if abortions were illegal for white women, they were unknown for Black women. They knew that Miss So-and-So did that but they also knew at least three people who had gone to Miss So-and-So and one who had died and one who couldn't have any babies anymore, so they were scared off from that and that's all they knew.

I'm glad abortion is legal now because of the physical danger that people went through. I don't know if it changes how one is going to react emotionally. If my mind-set is to do this because it's what I have to do, it's going to be the same whether it's legal or illegal. If one is ambivalent about whether it's the right thing to do, it's going to be the same whether it's legal or illegal. We hear a lot of women who go through great emotional agony, and I really sympathize and acknowledge that agony about their abortions. But at least having it legal takes away the physical stuff.

I didn't feel that I had committed an irreversible crime, considering what that child's life would have been like if it had been born with an unhappy mother. I felt that I would not have been the best mother I could be. I have a son now. I think I'm a great mom and I think he's a superior person because I chose to have him when I had him. He was a chosen child.

I did not feel the child would have been getting the best if I had allowed him to be. And I didn't feel that a four-week fetus had reached that being. So that made it easier for me because my child would have been Black, and Black kids don't get adopted. I would have been condemning my child to a life in an institution. I would not do that to a child. I think the child—and I put this in terms of God—understood . . . why I was doing what I was doing. I was not ready to be a good mother. It was a mistake. I had not wanted to be a mom. If I had been casual and not used any contraception ever, and been very casual about my sex, that's another thing I would have had to have dealt with. I felt that I had attempted very seriously to have "planned parenthood," and had slipped up because of David's bedroom and that one wild moment. So I felt comfortable making this decision. I wanted to be an educated mom, I wanted to be a mom in a certain economic situation before the kid came. I wanted to be a mom who felt culturally comfortable with her kid, and so I have no guilt, and I still feel that I did the right thing.

Anita

A lithe, athletic forty-six-year-old woman who appears to be in her early thirties. She is married, no children. Her background is professional nursing, and she currently works in New Jersey as a nursing consultant.

She speaks in a matter-of-fact way, straightforward and without undue emotion, about the events of twenty-three years ago.

It was during the summer, because it was warm. That's right, yes, it was warm weather. I went to a physician for a pregnancy test and he told me I was, I guess, I don't even remember, I was already close to twelve weeks. I asked him if he knew . . . uh . . . I wasn't in the position to have the child, was there any place he knew of where I could have an abortion? He said, "No," and counseled me to continue with the pregnancy. And that was that. That was my last contact with him. I went on to change gynecologists, and from then on I've used women ever since.

After I left the doctor's office I was so upset. But it's like everything else, you deal with it. All I remember is hearing that I was pregnant, being upset by that. I do remember crying, not wanting to be in that position, and angry with myself for allowing it to have happened. I saw James that very night and told him, and we decided that this was not the time, nor were we in a position to get married and have the baby. He said he would find someone to do an abortion. I didn't know anybody, I didn't know what to do. It was a very new and frightening thing for me. I'm sure there were people that had abortions but I didn't even ask. I wasn't in the position to sit down and discuss . . . This was when I first came to New York. I was here all by myself. I was living in the dorm (at the hospital) and the only person that I really became friendly with was Sally, who later became my roommate, and we were new friends. I just did not feel comfortable sitting down and talking with her about it, and I don't think she could have handled it anyway. She wasn't together herself.

Meanwhile, there was a doctor in Harlem who was doing abortions, and I got his name I guess through James, and I went there. I drove down the street that he lived on and there were a lot of these raunchy-looking people standing about outside, and of course, here I am, this young girl, you know. Whether they knew what was going on I don't know, but I didn't have the guts, I just didn't have the guts to stop the car and go in. I just left. I rode down the street and I looked, and I saw his office, and uh, I left. I couldn't do it. I didn't go in the building; it was too scary. And then we found this woman.

James found this gal who was—I'm not sure that she was a registered nurse—she had worked in a gynecologist's office. She may have been an aide, a nurse's aide. I met her before she did it, and she was really very nice. I felt very comfortable with her. I went and met her. It might have been in a diner or something like that. She lived in Harlem. I don't remember much else than that, other than going up to her apartment, and she had a lovely apartment, but again, going up into Harlem alone was a very scary thing to do, but what happens is that you have no choice; this is your only choice.

She was a lovely gal; she was very, very pleasant and she . . . The apartment was clean. There were roaches, I remember seeing a roach, everybody had roaches in New York. It wasn't unusual.

The scariest part was going up there, parking the car, going up into the apartment by myself. I can remember lying down in her bed in her bedroom facing out a window. There was a lot of light. She had a flashlight and she put on rubber gloves she had washed. What she used had been sterilized. She boiled it. Boiled the catheter and inserted it and put in some saline and that was it. I was there for a matter of maybe a couple of hours, just to make sure that it was beginning to work.

I left and I went back to James' place, and I aborted that night. I had a lot of cramps, but it wasn't excruciating pain. I was more frightened than anything else, and I think that made it rough to go through, not knowing what was happening.

James was a strange guy in the sense that he had a lot of trouble dealing with my pain. I guess he really cared and he just didn't know how to deal with it. At one point, uh, later in the relationship he drew some blood just to do a routine blood test for me and he was a nervous wreck. He could not draw the blood. He was so upset by sticking a needle into my arm and drawing the blood that I had to have someone else come and do it. At the time I was having the contractions, I could see that he was upset, but he wasn't really very verbal. He tried to calm me down a couple of times because I was getting very excited. I remember crying and he was very comforting. Finally I aborted. James took care of it. He wrapped it up and put it down the incinerator. Not a very pleasant experience.

He paid her, I don't remember how much it was. Probably about one hundred dollars, I guess, something like that.

But he certainly did not accompany me at any time. He was a doctor, from Liberia, and he didn't want to jeopardize his license or whatever. He didn't want to have any involvement that might reflect on him.

Luckily it worked out well. Luckily I went to the kind of person I went to, rather than to someone who was going to do a D&C and risk sticking the instrument right through my uterus. I felt very lucky.

It was a very difficult situation at that time. It was 1964, and abortion was illegal, and who could you trust? And where were you going to get the support that you were looking for from someone else? If you confided in someone were they going to support you and keep it quiet, and deal with it privately and not divulge what you had said? You didn't know. There were very few options for me at that time.

OUT OF WEDLOCK

"The most deadly of all possible sins is the mutilation of a child's spirit. There can be nothing more destructive to a child's spirit than being unwanted, and there are few things more disruptive to a woman's spirit than being forced without love or need into motherhood."

—Erik Erikson

Dee

Dee lives in Colorado with her husband and twenty-year-old son. Although she very much wanted to tell her story, Dee was clearly shaken by the intensity of her own feelings; she was frequently overcome by sadness. Often hesitating, her voice would fade into silence. . . .

The way I got pregnant was really "social rape," I think you would call it . . . but I thought it was my fault. I was working, and I became friendly with a group of people, and I went out with them a lot, but it was always like a gang going out. I sort of got paired with Johnny, and we spent a lot of time together, and, and . . . [voice shaking] I had no reason to feel or believe that he would force himself on me.

We had gone out dancing and wound up at Johnny's apartment, and it was very late. The others left, and Johnny was supposed to drive me home, which he always did, but . . . But he decided not to . . . I thought it was my fault. I felt that I— we had been out, we had been dancing, fairly seductive dances, I thought, and I thought that I had aroused this passion in him that was uncontrollable, so . . . I resisted, but it didn't matter. He pushed me down on that black couch . . .

So, after . . . afterward, I was really worried and afraid, because you lived with terror. And then I found out I was pregnant.

When you got pregnant at that time, let's see, I was born in

1932, so this was 1952 . . . I did go to a doctor to confirm whether or not I was pregnant. A girlfriend of mine had a doctor in Virginia she went to, so I went to him too. He gave me a shot; I guess it was a "morning after" shot. He said if you were not pregnant, it would bring on your period, and if you were pregnant, there was nothing anyone could do about it. It didn't work.

It's so hard. I've never spoken about this to anybody, or certainly not in this detail.

I was twenty when this happened. You see, Bob, the man I was in love with, was in the Army. I had been dating him since I was fifteen. I was very much in love and we had been sexually active. Before he left, I wanted to have a more committed relationship, but he thought we should see other people. That's why I was going out with this group.

When Bob came home on leave, I called and told him I was pregnant, and he was devastated. He was Catholic. He was full of tremendous contempt and I certainly could understand a lot of why he was angry, but I felt abandoned. He couldn't handle that I had gotten pregnant, in any way, form, shape; and with another man! . . . And I never told the truth of what had happened.

To say that you were raped, to me was a very shameful thing. And also, I didn't feel that I had been raped. In retrospect, I realize that's what happened, but then I thought that the only definition of rape was you were walking down the street and someone you didn't know accosted you, or climbed in your window. If you knew someone and you wound up having intercourse with that person, it was the woman's responsibility. That was in the thirties and forties when I was growing up. So it never dawned on me that I had been anything other than provocative and unfaithful.

It never occurred to me to have an abortion. There was no place that you could go that was safe, that I knew of in the social strata that I was in. The only thing you knew were back alley stories. There was no place . . . there wasn't anything I could do about it. I think there were doctors who did it, but I didn't know how to find them, and nobody I knew did either, except my mother, possibly, and she never said anything about it. Later on there was a story . . . My father had died of cancer when my mother was pregnant, and she tells the story about going to Dr. Jenkins, who suggested performing an abortion on her. So, she had the knowledge that Dr. Jenkins performed abortions, but she never passed it on to me. I never ever really verbalized that before.

I told Johnny and my family, and everybody's solution was for us to get married. I had quit my job, and I was living at home. One night I was watching television, and "Blossoms in the Dust" came on. This was the story of a woman who got pregnant out of wedlock and decided to have her baby and not get married. There was a place in Milwaukee where she went, where many women went—this was a story I heard all my life, growing up. You would wind up working in the laundry or something like that to pay your way. They wouldn't let you come until you were in your seventh month, which meant that everyone would know your condition. Edna Gladney changed the laws in Texas to protect children who were born out of wedlock, so that it did not say "bastard" on their birth certificate. And there was secrecy for the mother as well. So a woman could come and have that child and no one would know. The homes that the children went into were really lovely homes . . . And I called them! I was just three months pregnant, but I explained the circumstances: I desperately needed to come there, so they said, "Come on."

I told my family, and they were totally hysterical. How could I give up the flesh of our family? There were giant scenes with Johnny pounding on the door trying to get into the house, screaming it was his baby . . . how dare I . . .

I didn't have the fare to fly to Texas, and I had no way of getting there. I had pitted my will against the family and they knew that I wasn't going to change my mind. So my brothers told me they would take care of the fare.

I knew I would never be able to love that child the way it needed to be loved. I felt it was an innocent that didn't have anything to do with what was going on.

And so I went to the Gladney home, and spent six months of my life . . . It changed my life. It changed my self-image. The women who ran the Gladney home were so kind to me. There were, let's see how many of us— There was Judy and Elaine and Pat and Gwen—and so the four of us, and also the others, Lydia and Irene, we all arrived within a two- or three-week period. It was dormitory style, and what we expected to find, you know, was a conclave of whores, and each of us would be the one nice person there. But what we found was each other. A handful of women abandoned by society, in a bizarre place, safe from the world—this was Fort Worth, Texas.

I was lucky being in a place where you were cherished, feeling that you would be allowed to go back to your own life as a whole person. They did a wonderful thing, because it prepared me to let go of that child. And wonderful things happened to me there. I began to think of myself as an intellectual . . . I was very beautiful when I was young, and I always saw that as a commodity, because that was a value that was placed on women. I began to think of women with a kind of tenderness that comes from being part of a group of women who have been shown very clearly the vulnerability and helplessness of being a woman, and who have chosen within the structure of society to live a different way. Judy, who is still a good friend, had gone all the way through trying to find someone to do an abortion, and had every story one could tell. With the exception of Judy, and one older woman who had older children, all of us were there because of an experience that was to some degree against our will. For me to get away from my family, and have people view me aside from being part of a family, was wonderful. What changed my life was to really take charge of my life. And that was my story . . .

I had the baby; it was a little boy.

When I came home . . . I had a terrible experience going

home [crying, her voice shaking]. I missed my plane. The woman who made reservations told me it was . . . twelve at night, and the plane actually left at twelve that afternoon. I couldn't get another flight our of Fort Worth for days, and I needed to get out of there. I went and spent the night in a hotel and took a train home the next day, which in a way was probably good because it was a two-day trip and gave me that time, but . . . [voice shaking] there were a lot of soldiers on the train, and I still looked beautiful, and it was maybe eight or ten days after I'd had the baby. I was still tired and going through all the hormonal changes, and I couldn't handle anyone making a pass at me. But this soldier sat next to me and fell asleep on my shoulder. I felt so violated . . . but I was still not able to say, "Go away."

I was very afraid of men for a long time; I was afraid, I felt spoiled and very threatened.

I came home, and . . . my mother never spoke to me about it, for the whole rest of her life. You know, I spent the last six or seven weeks of my mother's life with her, in the room with her when she was dying, and we never spoke about it, but my brother—I had dinner with my brother one night and he said, "She never got over not seeing that child." By then I just . . . I told him that it wasn't their issue, that child! That child was mine, and I had made the decision that I needed to make about it.

But I do know one thing. My mother trusted only me to make the decisions at the end of her life. I feel it was because she felt, always, from the day I made the decision about the baby and she knew that no one was going to change my position, that I could be trusted. Very paradoxical, but of all her children, I, who resisted her the most, wound up really protecting her in the end . . . because I had learned early on where you take control of your life.

When I came home I felt completely isolated. I had come from this intense experience, a re-viewing of myself as not a bad person, but a person that other people were attracted to, and I had found my own intellectual self, and . . . I came back into this atmosphere . . . of . . . of . . . a certain kind of ignorance. It was a different life view. I had no friends.

I saw Bob when I came home, and it was really still a very bitter experience for me. I could see very easily that there would be no repairing that relationship. I felt I would have to find someone in my life; that I would be pretty worthless if I didn't find and make a good marriage . . . and that it would have to be based on honesty.

I met Sam very soon afterward, and we started a relationship. About the third or fourth time I went out with him, I told him about the child, and it was no big deal to him. Sam really wanted to get married. As it got closer and I felt more pressure to really set a date, I broke up with him. In the aftermath of the delivery and the adoption and the coming home and the loss of Bob and all that—it happened in such a compressed amount of time—I came from that protected situation back into the real world, and I didn't want to get married. I didn't want to . . . I just wanted to be left alone.

That summer my sister got married and there was something about the men at that wedding, and I thought . . . I can't let Sam go. I love him and I'm not going to find anybody like him again in my life . . .

We had Deborah three years after we were married. I had a miscarriage before Deborah, which was really sad; I was almost nine months pregnant. I felt like that was punishment. You see, having had that child and giving it up for adoption had a tremendous effect on my life. Because of the guilt about that, I'd bring waifs home, homeless children. We've had a series of kids that would come and stay four or five months at a time. In a strange way, intuitively or whatever, each one of my children at one time or another would become very attached to waifs. When Deborah was fifteen I told her about the child . . . and my reasons for getting so involved with homeless, orphaned children. After I told her there seemed to be more freedom of choice with her life. It wasn't until I had Noah, who is now twenty, that I really had the full of impact of what happened. That rape is rape. And how I really did get pregnant. I had that tremendous burden of having no choice, just nothing to do but have that child. It was just tremendously painful to have to remember the whole thing.

It really comes down to women as chattel; a woman is property. That must have been what offended Bob the most. He once said to me, "What did I ever do to hurt you that you would do something like this to me?" I never said it to Bob. I never said it to Sam. I never told Sam until Deborah was almost nine and a half, after Noah was born, so we had been married thirteen years when I figured out that I had been raped and that it wasn't my fault . . . I felt all of that time, that if you behave in a sexual manner in any way, shape, or form, and then the man goes out of control, it's the woman's responsibility. That's what I was taught. It was really a woman's responsibility to say no, because men just didn't have the capacity. That once they were aroused to a certain point that was it. In other words, I was playing with fire and I got burned. And that is really the position that I took.

Women of my era were raised by our Victorian mothers, and we are our mothers' daughters. We judge ourselves with their eyes, and so I don't know that we could be anything else but silent. And I'm glad I'm not going to be anymore.

Deborah

Deborah is Dee's daughter. She is a journalist who has authored a book about well-known women.

It was Deborah who offered to arrange the interview with her mother. As she was describing her mother's struggle to cope with having given up a child for adoption, she began to tell her own story about the "second-generation effects" of her mother's experience.

First, I should probably give you a little bit of the context in which I found out about my mother's experience. I was about fourteen, I think, and I was having a relationship with a boy who was maybe sixteen or seventeen at the time. It was a sexual relationship—it was during the seventies and a lot of women were sleeping with men quite early. I don't know whether or not my mother actually knew I was sleeping with this boy, but she did know that we were becoming very, very involved with each other and I think she was a little bit worried, you know, about our seriousness at that age, the serious nature the relationship was taking on.

About eight or nine months into the relationship, I began to feel that I wanted to get out of it, and I was beginning to feel very trapped. He himself was adopted and felt very, very strongly excluded by his family, even though I suppose his parents really did love him. He had a very brutal and brutalizing father who was very macho. He had been a Marine in World

War II, and was always telling war stories. He was a very cold and domineering man. And I was quite afraid to break up with his son, because he had a very strong temper like his father. I had some very deep, almost physical fears of what would happen to me if I hurt this boy, or if I stopped this relationship. I think my mother all the time was sort of observing this, and at some point decided to tell me her experience, because she felt that somehow her having given up a child for adoption—who was a boy child—was somehow making me feel more tied to this person than I perhaps would have been if she hadn't experienced that. She really had taken this boy that I was seeing into the family.

So she told me . . . one night I was up late watching TV and she came into the living room and she told me exactly what happened to her. She told me that when she was a young woman she had been raped, and that her family didn't believe that she had been raped, and that she became pregnant as a result of this, and that she had to leave her family and go have the child. She had had quite a long relationship with another man whom she had always dreamt she would marry, you know, a sort of childhood sweetheart. Having this experience of the rape and having a child and putting the child up for adoption had done so much damage to the relationship that it could never be the same between them, and his parents would never accept her. She told me, along with that story, about how she felt toward my boyfriend. You see, she really had taken my boyfriend into the family. As she explained, she saw in him the son that she had—so long ago—given up, and in a very real sense, lost. She realized that by nurturing my boyfriend, by making him a part of our family—a far less brutal family than he happened to have been placed in as an adopted child—she was acting on and expressing her own wishes to nurture the child that she had had to give up. She said she wanted me to know because she wanted me to be free to break up with him. She also told me that she would protect me, because she understood that I was afraid of his anger. He was quite violent in a lot of ways. He was harassing me, saying, "If you ever break up with me, I will kill myself." My mother really impressed on me that you can't stay with someone just because they don't have enough life will of their own; you can't live someone's life for them. You can't save someone from their own destructive impulses. She made me feel very strong about that, explaining to me that even if he did wind up doing things that were self-destructive, it wouldn't be my fault. It was a very empowering thing for me, and I did wind up breaking up with him.

This was right at the end of the summer before I was to enter high school. He had just graduated high school, but a lot of his friends were still there. He really did cause trouble for me. I had the experience of going into high school for the first time, and having all of his boyfriends call me slut and whore. I mean, that was everyone's impression of me. They would follow me down the hallways at school and yell that. It made me feel very marginal. It made me feel like I couldn't make friends. I was stigmatized. I ended up running in a rough crowd, because that was the crowd that was accepting of me.

I did have a repeating pattern of being attracted to young men who felt they had no future or no family—waifs. They just weren't grounded or stable young men. And I think that was probably also an effect of my mother's experience. I don't know quite how. Even though I got the actual information at thirteen, it still took me until my twenties to stop doing that. She still does have a tendency to take waifs into the house. My brother's present girlfriend is a girl who's been sort of rejected by her family, and she's now living with my family, and she's become a daughter to them. So it's not a pattern that's broken by the actual telling of the tale; I don't think that that's quite enough. In a lot of ways, I also see my father not really allowing my mother to resolve those conflicts. I feel that . . . when, for instance, I told my mother about your wanting to interview her and my father was present, he said, "I don't want some half-wit kid turning up on my doorstep." So, obviously he has a lot of ambivalence, and obviously it took a lot of courage for her to go ahead and do this sort of interview. He's a very kind and very gentle man, but these issues obviously get his hackles up. I feel like he probably really wanted her to bury the past, and he wants to act in some way as if having a child, bringing a child into the world that was an unwanted child, is something that a woman can just forget. That it's something very clinical . . . that the baby was born, and the connection was severed. I don't think he quite understands that giving birth to a child is an emotional experience. Even in the circumstances of the child conceived in rape, I think women are able to still forge a connection with that child, separate from the act of violence that caused the conception. I think that my father is unwilling to take a look at the lifelong effect on my mother: that she still does this sort of thing, constantly bringing in waifs . . . homeless children, children in trouble. I think that she has a very altruistic personality, but there's no other reason that it had to take that particular form.

I give my mother a lot of credit. She has worked hard to be aware of the subtle influence of her past, and the effects it might have had on her children.

It could have been a lot more traumatic for me if my mother hadn't dealt with these issues so openly. I have a great deal of respect for her. It has taken a great deal of courage for her to do that.

Margot

Margot is a registered nurse who has written several books
on pregnancy and birth, and she has worked as a Lamaze
instructor.
  We are talking in her Brooklyn apartment, looking out
over the water at the Statue of Liberty.

First of all, I had three abortions, but the first one was the most
hard-hitting. I was nineteen. I had gone to one year of college,
and I didn't like it, and I didn't want to go back. I only went
because I didn't know what else to do with myself. My main
ambition was to get married and be taken care of. My father
said, "While you're waiting for a husband, you're not just going
to sit at home—you're going to get yourself a career, so what do
you want to do?" And having absolutely no sense of myself as a
person at all, I said, "Well, what do women do?" They're either
secretaries, nurses, or teachers, and I didn't want to do the other
two, so I chose nursing. I wasn't really choosing nursing 'cause I
was crazy about it—it was just because it was the lesser of three
evils that were open to women. My father checked around with
some doctor friends and discovered this little hospital in Maine
that did have a practical nursing school, and it never occurred
to me to go to a higher level. The women who were there were
Vermont country girls. You had to be a high school graduate
and that's all. And I had a year of college and I was an upper-
class WASP from New York. The teachers at the school were

also Vermont backwoods women, and I was a real misfit there. I never thought particularly well of myself wherever I was. So that wasn't anything new to me. But those were the particular conditions of my being a misfit there.

I was going out with a guy who was at an Ivy League College on the G.I. Bill. He was twenty-seven. He'd been in the Navy during the second World War. He was a fraternity man, one of the Dekes. He was one of the guys. I thought he was wonderful looking and a man of the world. I met him when I worked as a waitress at the Hanover Inn, and he was the bartender there. He was Catholic. We were officially engaged. We had had an announcement in the paper done à la upper class. It came out in *The New York Times*. I had a diamond. My parents didn't like him, but they didn't say much about it. We used to screw in the front seat of his car. And it was really, for me, a way of being held and getting attention. And he would interrupt intercourse. And I felt like I was getting my love interrupted, so I asked him not to do that, and so I got pregnant. My parents would've just been . . . they always thought I was trashy because of these experiences that I had had with men when I was a kid. I was sexually abused, and they felt I had engineered it, when I was six and eight. I was spanked for it and they felt that I was a dirty, you know, a dirty little girl, so of course I was a dirty grown-up. I knew I would get a large dose of that, and anyway, what good would it do if I went and told them I was pregnant?

But in the middle of being overwhelmed and frightened, there was another part of me which was tremendously excited—I mean very happy. I was elated. And I begged Tom to get married. I said, "We're engaged—let's just get married." I would quit nursing school. By this time he was working as a traveling salesman, and he was always somewhere close enough that I could go on a bus and be with him for two days, and sort of pretend to housekeep. That was what I desperately wanted—to make a little home. Tom said to me he absolutely could not get married this way because it would kill his parents if they knew what he was doing. That was his Catholic mentality. And years later when I was talking with a guy that I was going out with and told him this, he raised my consciousness by saying, "He didn't worry about it killing his parents when he was screwing you." And somewhere that touched a real anger in me, but I couldn't admit it for at least ten years. I had chosen myself a guy who was irresponsible as far as my welfare was concerned.

Then he had to track down an abortionist. He did all these little things in code. He talked to a pharmacist that he knew and he'd say, "You know, I have a ship that is now full of cargo. Do you know any way to . . ." And the right person, he figured— and it was true—would understand this code and say, "Oh yeah, I've heard of these ships, and I do know people who un-load them and I'll check for you." I read some letters he'd re-ceived from a friend. He apparently had written him, and in the same kind of lingo, the friend had written back, "I hope that that ship disposed of its cargo by now." I mean, that's pretty tawdry. But I felt tawdry, and it never occurred to me to protest it. Meanwhile at nursing school, I was very rapidly losing my waistline. I told two girls in my class, who were sort of delighted with this secret, which they were seeing as a little soap opera. They were supportive as far as they could be, but you know, I needed really—adult support and counseling. But again, it didn't occur to me that I deserved it. I thought I was doing pretty well that there were a couple of girls who at least didn't condemn me. I was very scared and very alone there in this nursing school with nobody knowing what was going on with me except for them.

Finally, Tom found a genuine M.D. who did abortions, who had this whole rigamarole set up. One of the weekends that I was off, Tom came and picked me up, and we drove to Boston. We had to drive very fast because we had to get there at a cer-tain hour. This doctor had said, "If you're not there on the dot of seven, I'm leaving, and don't bother to try to make another appointment with me. We either do it or we don't." So there was this pressure. I felt like I was going on this adventure that was sort of exciting. I really didn't know what they did. Lurking in the back of my mind, I had some very deep fear about my life, which no conscious part of me recognized because I really couldn't have handled it. It would have undone me. We went to a hotel in Boston. Tom had registered in advance. This doctor came up to the room at a certain hour, examined me and said, "Yes, you are pregnant." Tom hid out in the bathroom. And then the doctor said, "Okay, this is what I want you to do. I want you to go to a certain address," and he named it. "There is a garage there, it will be closed down. My car will be there." He said to me—I mean it was like a spy story—"I want you to pull up. I want you to get out of the car. I want you to walk purposefully, do not look around—do not look as though you are skulking or hiding—just get right out and walk purposefully over to the car which will be parked there. It's a blue car. Just get right into the passenger's side, just do it, bingo—1,2,3. And then I will take you to the place where this is going to be done. And I will deliver you back to the same garage. And I want you"—to Tom—"to be there to pick her up. And I want you to stay there." "How much time is it going to take?" Tom asked. I think Tom was beginning at that point to realize that maybe he would never see me again. Maybe, you know, he was sending me to my death.

Let me tell you something—I was so desperately, from the beginning of my life, in need of attention of any kind, that this was attention to me. And I said, "How long is it going to take?" The doctor said, "I have no idea and I don't want you looking at any watches." So we did this whole plan. When I was in his car, he explained to me that we were going to go to a residential neighborhood where there were houses very close together on both sides of the street. We were going to park in a place which would be empty—right in front of a house—he was going to get out and go in. I was to look at my watch, or the clock in the car—and in exactly six and a half minutes, or some set time, I was to get out of the car exactly as though I lived there—again purposefully—walk right up the walk, open the door and go in. "Act as though you've been on this street twenty thousand times." And I did that. I walked into a little downstairs apartment that had a hall that stretched right ahead with some rooms off it that went right back to a kitchen. There was a nice smell of soup on the stove. It was somebody's home, very similar to the kind Tom lived in. Lower class but comfortable and cozy. And a woman came out of the room directly on the left. She was exactly what you'd expect—overweight in a housedress—pleasant face—and she rather brusquely said, "Come with me"—and I walked down the hall to a bathroom. There was a douche bag hanging on the closet door, which stank to me of Clorox—and she said—"I want you to douche with this and then come directly into the room." I went into the bedroom, with a double bed in it. There was a rubber sheet on it. I was asked to lie down and bring my rear end to the edge of the bed and the doctor then put this sling around my legs, and around my neck. I've seen pictures of them—of these things in books on deliveries in less sophisticated countries for home deliveries. It's just a piece of canvas—like a belt that goes around your neck and on the outside of your legs and under your knees and back. And you can relax and this thing supports you. I was kind of interested in what he was going to do and wanted to be cooperative and congenial and somewhat sophisticated; being a nurse I would know these things—except I didn't know anything, and I really wasn't a nurse. And he brought up a pail—a great metal pail that clanked. And pulled the edge of this rubber sheet down into it. And the woman sat down on the bed to my right. Then he started scraping and I got really bad cramps, you know, it really hurt. And he said to me, "You must not move. Don't you dare move," because obviously if I moved he would slip and cut me. I didn't know even what a curette looked like. I just sort of pictured a knife. I guess my idea that he was scraping me with a straight razor was probably useful in keeping me still. But it hurt so much that I started to get nauseated and I said, "I'm going to throw up," and he said, "No, you're not." And all the time that I was talking and he was answering me, he was working. And in the middle of this—my feeling so sick and in pain—another part of me was appreciating that he was continuing to work, right through it, that his main reason for being there was to do this job and to do it well.

Somewhere along the line there, the front door opened, and that was directly outside the hall from the room we were in. He said, "Who the hell was that?" to the woman. And she said, "Oh, it's just somebody." And he said, "Well, he better damn well not come in here." And she said, "Don't worry." And again I was impressed. I would have expected him to jump up—run into the closet—but he didn't, he just kept right on working. I had the sense that if the police had marched in he would say, "Okay, you can take me, but I'm going to finish this job." Tom felt he was in it for the money. I'm sure he was, but I think there was some kind of social conscience going with him. I had a sense that he was making a ton of money, but I remember his saying in the car on the way there that it really was disgusting that women should have to come out and have abortions like this.

It hurt me so much—it was that sickening kind of pain that comes when you have cramps. I really couldn't lie still—but I had to lie still, so I had to do something else instead of move— so I started to say the Lord's Prayer out loud—at a rapid pace. I'm not religious. I don't believe in the Lord's Prayer; I never go to church. That was what came to me instead of "The Star-Spangled Banner"—or God knows what else—or counting, and I think I had some vague idea that maybe God would protect me. Although I would have said I don't believe in God.

And that threw him. I was very intuitive about everything that was going on, very sensitive about all the nuances, and there was a break in his rhythm, the merest break. I knew that he was thinking, "What the fuck have I got here; God damn, sitting there saying the Lord's Prayer." Anyway, I just said it over and over and over and oh, the woman held my hand. I must have squeezed her fingers into nothing. And she held my hand back, and gave me strength that way. Poor little soul: This strange woman who had sat by all these God knows how many numbers of women having abortions, held my hand.

Well, afterward, I had to walk really straight to the car and act as though nothing had happened. The doctor left me with Tom, who was frightened that something had happened to me but really basically concerned with himself. When we got back to the hotel, he went to sleep immediately with this terrible headache. The next day Tom drove me back to nursing school.

Then, maybe a year or so later, we decided to get married. Sort of on the spur of the moment. On the morning we were supposed to do it, I just didn't bother to get up. We were staying at my family's house and Tom slept in another room, of course, so he finally came up to see what I was doing at ten o'clock in the morning still in bed. He said, "I had a feeling you don't really want to get married," and I said, "You're right." Although it was terribly hard for me to say that. Years later, when I met him again, I saw he really was a kind of sleazy salesman type. I made the right decision.

Within a year after that, I slept with somebody and found I was pregnant. I was living in New York in a really grubby apartment in a terribly grubby building. My self-esteem hadn't risen any by then. I was doing private duty nursing. I had gotten my LPN. I was living alone. I had no steady boyfriend. I called a friend of mine to ask if she knew anyone. I knew she's had a baby—she'd gotten pregnant and had the baby—she'd gone to one of these homes. And I asked her if she knew anything about abortions and she didn't. I didn't really know how to find an abortionist. I couldn't see myself going into pharmacies and doing that code trip that Tom had done. She said to me, "Look—it's no big deal. You just go along and wear a girdle, a really tight girdle, and loose sweaters and things, until you can't cover it up anymore, and then you just go off to a home." She said, "It's not particularly nice, but it's not terrible either. You just stay there for three months." So I figured that would be my plan—and I kept on doing private duty nursing. I always worked at night, so that I wasn't terribly visible. I wore huge, loose sweaters and a very tight Playtex girdle—it never occurred to me what I'd be doing to the baby. I was totally unaware of anatomy, even after this training that I'd now been through, and somewhere about, I think, my fifth month I began to get incredible cramps, and they'd be so bad they'd make me very light-headed. I would have to sit down immediately wherever I was and put my head down. I used to go into stores and just say, "I need somewhere to sit down." I didn't look pregnant so they wouldn't know that. They'd just think, "God, this woman is going to pass out." And I'd sit down—completely alone in this. I guess I was just used to being alone, being lonely and alone and unsupported. I got scared because of these cramps. And I decided I needed a doctor, and I did then the first assertive thing I had done in my whole life. I looked up in the yellow pages "Unwed Mothers." I called some agency in the city. I admitted to the woman who answered that I was an unmarried mother, figuring she would say, you scum and all kinds of stuff—but she didn't. She referred me to another agency that gave you doctors' names, depending on what your ailment is. I called and I got a woman on the phone, and I said, "I would like an obstetrician," and she said, "All right, where do you live? I'll give you one that's easy for you to get to." I said, "Well, I'm not married, and I would just like somebody who's really nice." It makes me want to cry even when I tell this. I fully expected her to say, "Oh, how disgusting," or something, and to my total astonishment, she said, "Good for you for being so honest. I really respect you. I have a woman doctor and I think she'd be very nice." This was the first time in my life that I exposed myself purposefully and somebody stepped forward and met me. Anyway, I went to this woman doctor. She said I was fine, and she then sat me down in her office and I told her I wasn't married. Part of me was saying—listen—fuck you, world—I'm going to step right out there and I'm not going to pretend. I'm pregnant. This is me right now. Pregnant me. And she said, "Well, do you want to keep this baby?" And I said, "No." I don't know how she introduced it, but she said, "I have a couple who are looking to adopt a baby. Would you be willing to make an arrangement with them? They will pay for you to go wherever you want to go for your last months, they'll pay all your medical expenses and they will pay for me, in return for taking the baby." She explained to me that it was not illegal, and she explained what I would have to do in terms of going to their lawyer and signing something before finishing the pregnancy. I would then have three months to change my mind afterward. And at that time, I would be expected to go back and sign the baby over for good. And I said, "Yes."

I must say that the lawyer treated me like shit. But God, people were so out of it in those days. That was the mid-fifties, you know. The doctor never alluded in any way to my emotional state—ever. And in fact, at one point in the pregnancy she had it all worked out. She said, "I want you to come exactly at five after ten o'clock," so I would be in the back and they would be in the waiting room. She called them into her office, and we all shook hands, and I was supposed to have some sort of proof that they actually had a bona fide home. They showed me some pictures of the house they were building. The woman couldn't have babies. She was sweet. He was very kind. And I said at the end of the interview, "I'm really glad you're going to have my baby."

At any rate, I started going out with the man I eventually married around that time. And sleeping with him. And somewhere along the line he said, "I notice you haven't had a period. Have you gotten pregnant?" I said, "Yes, but it's not yours. I was pregnant before I met you." And he was devastated by that. He was a very sweet, very responsible man. And I felt like a real heel. He did feel very sorry for me, felt somehow I'd been taken advantage of. He offered to come live with me. I moved into a residential hotel on the West Side to spend the last months of my pregnancy. I got a room with a little balcony. I was due at the beginning of July, but I was three weeks late. The wild thing was that we never, ever discussed the pregnancy. We'd look at the baby moving, but we never discussed it. Somewhere when I was going into that overdue period, the lawyer called me up in my hotel room and said, "When are you going to have this baby anyway?" And I said, "I don't know," and he said, "Well, you know, they can't just keep on paying these bills forever."

At the time, I felt pretty lucky—I had this guy staying with me, I was in a nice hotel. I went out, you know, and bought groceries and cooked for us and I, at last, was making my little nest in a very strange and sad way.

I started with those little tiny contractions which are tiny things, nowhere near coming up to what I felt with the abortion. And I thought, Oh, I can handle this. It was about eleven in the evening and we took a taxi to the hospital. Now, he was really also very spaced out, because he left me at the door, and when I got upstairs the doctor said, "Is your friend going to join you?" And I said, "No, he's gone home." And it just didn't occur to him to say that he would come in with me. And I actually married this guy and never, ever talked to him about that pregnancy, ever.

It was a tiny little private hospital. There was one nurse who sat at a desk doing records. It got uncomfortable and I got scared. It began to hurt, and I began to grind my teeth as a way to—like the Lord's Prayer had been. And she turned around—it was the only time I remember this nurse speaking to me. And she said, "Don't do that. That drives me crazy."

I was lying flat on my back in this bed with side rails, and I felt very lonely and again, as with the first pregnancy, thought about my mother. But there's no way I could've ever called her. My mother was also so naive and so innocent at the time, I didn't think she could handle it. She would not have known how to support me. She would've gone to my father who would've treated me like scum, which I already felt like. I had sort of little flashes, then I'd realize that I was having a baby and nobody knew about it: That was terribly lonely. I had told my parents that I was on this private duty case in the country with some woman, and that I was really busy and that's why they weren't hearing from me. This is all very sad, you know, that you couldn't go to your own parents about something. And my mother never did know. And my kids don't know that I had this baby.

The doctor came in and she leaned on the side rails and she

said, "How are you doing?" And I said—and this is with an
enormous effort because I did not believe that I deserved anything—I said, "I wish you'd stay with me." I think I took her
hand, and she put my hand back in the bed, patted it, and said,
"Oh, you're going to be fine. We're all right down the hall if
you need anything." And the point is, of course, that nobody
thought about emotional support. And I don't know that people
thought about that anyway in those days. If I needed anything—what did that mean? If I started hemorrhaging or something weird? . . .

I still had my eyes shut. I was still under the anesthesia—
almost at the point where I wasn't able to open them yet—and
somebody said to me, "It's all over." And I didn't believe it.
They put my hand on my stomach and I was flat. And my first
reaction was, Thank God I didn't have to go through that anymore.

Anyway, the doctor came in and asked how I was, and said
the baby looked fine and was healthy. So I told the doctor I'd
like to see him. And she really questioned that. She was afraid
that I would become attached and cancel the whole adoption.
But I felt I owed it to the baby and to myself. So, the doctor said
"Okay" and the day that I was to go home, I went to see the
baby. I said, "He's very small" or something—I remember making some kind of comment like that, more for the sake of the
audience than anything I really felt. I think I felt intense embarrassment at this proof of my indiscretion. But, of course, that's
just a cover-up for deeper feelings. I do think at times—I had
Jonas a year later—I didn't really understand about loving anyone until my children were grown up, which was maybe eight
years ago. And this was twenty-five or thirty years ago.

During the next couple of days in the hospital, there was an
intern or a resident who used to come in all the time. He never
talked to me about the pregnancy or the baby. We would just
talk about anything. But he would sort of hang around with his
arms folded and he'd talk to me. And I had the distinct sense
that he was looking me over as an unwed mother—a phenome-

non that maybe he wouldn't meet anywhere else, and he wanted to get his fill of it. A male looking over the fallen woman trip. I really don't know how much of that I imagined, but I think I'm not wrong. There were several nurses who treated me that way.

There was one young nurse who was different, though. There was something in her attitude which was very supportive. She was very warm. She was very discreet, but she was there. She was wonderful to me.

When I went back for my postpartum checkup, the doctor said, "Oh, I thought you might like to know about Miss So-and-so. She killed herself. She found she was pregnant and she took an overdose." The nurse who had been so nice to me. I think she was Catholic and she couldn't face the guilt. She killed herself because she was pregnant. And the doctor thought I would like to know. That's a terrible thing to tell somebody, especially somebody who had just gone and given up a baby. What a depressing thing—the one nurse who was so nice to me.

Lucy

Lucy has a mission. You can't know her without knowing she's a pro-choice activist and why.

She helped to organize a ten-hour bus trip to Washington, D.C., to march for abortion rights. I was in Washington, too, distributing an author's query for interviews. Lucy's response was emphatic and immediate. She invited me to come and stay at her home in upstate New York; she scheduled five interviews in this remote rural area, and for two days she drove me from house to house. Her opening the way made it possible for me to talk with these women about the most intimate details of their lives.

She knows the connections between the issues of illegal abortion and its implications for herself and other women. To her, the denial of the right to choose abortion and the victimization of women are illustrated by what she went through. In her words, "I was trapped, but I got out. I escaped. I hope all of these stories really, really help. I want women to be free."

I'll start with my earliest knowledge about girls that got pregnant and what they did about it. The first person I knew who got pregnant was a woman I met when I was just out of high school. She was a pal of my sister's and she became pregnant: She met and fell in love with this Moroccan fellow and she got pregnant, but it was an impossible situation because this fellow hadn't planned on staying in the United States. He didn't even have a permanent visa. Somehow through the grapevine she heard about this doctor on Rivington Street, which was down in lower Manhattan near the Bowery, and I went down there with her. This was 1967 and he supposedly did abortions. We went there thinking everything would be taken care of, but he gave her these pills to take. It wasn't called pills to cause an abortion. It was called pills to bring on your period. She took these pills and he gave her a shot in her arm, and in about two days she got heavy cramps and her period was "brought on." We were very young, and we didn't know what it was. Maybe she was just late.

My sister went away to college, and she had about six months of college to go, and her boyfriend had already graduated and he was going into the service when she got pregnant. Now mind you, neither of these girls knew anything about birth control, or rhythm. We grew up in a place where nobody knew anything about these things and you were lucky if your mother told you where your period came from. So my sister got pregnant and she went to this doctor on Rivington Street, and it was in a tenement building in a dirty, filthy neighborhood in a dirty, filthy place and there were women lined up on benches on both sides of the room waiting for this doctor to treat them for pregnancy.

My sister went in there and had the same treatment that Pat had, and it didn't work, so she and her boyfriend decided they would get married. They didn't tell my parents she was pregnant but they told them they were getting married and my father said, "No way, I'm not giving you a wedding until you graduate from college." We were all very afraid of my father, so she just didn't argue about it and she went back to school and they both were old enough to get married without consent, and so they did it.

He went into the service—he was shipped off to Vietnam, and she lived with his family on whatever he was able to send her from his service pay.

They only had that one child, even though that child put pressure on them when he was about nine; he wanted a sister or a brother, but they never would. It worked out not so badly for her, but she went through a terrible emotional crisis. Of course when you got pregnant, you were a slut.

She never finished school. At that time, in the late sixties, you didn't stay in college if you were pregnant. She got on birth control after that. She had maybe twelve credits to go, but she became busy with her family life. While she lived with his parents, she was helping her mother-in-law with her own brood. Her mother-in-law had ten children. She was like the oldest daughter in the family.

Then my sister Sue was having trouble in school, quit school and got a job. Sue was a very strict Catholic. When she was about seventeen, she was introduced to a guy who was nine years older than she was. Well, eventually they began having a sexual relationship. But he wasn't practicing birth control, and she didn't know about it, so she just worried about it, and finally it happened that she became pregnant. She had to run away from home because she was so afraid of telling my father and dealing with his anger and hurting my mother, so she wrote a runaway note and she ran away. She was forced into marrying this guy because my father threatened him that if he didn't get a divorce from his previous marriage and marry his daughter within a certain period of weeks, he was going to turn him into the police department for cohabitation. So with no time to think about it they just—Zap! got married.

The point with both of my sisters was that they had no education and nobody told them anything. Everything was left to chance, and they were put in situations where marriage was the thing that was decided on because you were pregnant and you didn't have any other options to think about.

I can remember when both of my older sisters had children, that feeling of being competitive, the feeling of being left behind, that I wanted to marry and I wanted to have children.

I got married when I had just turned twenty-one, and I was

very naive. When I first met my husband-to-be, I did go to a doctor and I did get birth control pills and my future husband Paul found out I was taking them, and he made me throw them away. In his mind, he thought that if I was on birth control pills, that meant I could go to bed with anybody I wanted to and I'd never get pregnant. Therefore, birth control pills give girls the opportunity to be promiscuous! So he made me throw them away, and I did. Because I was a young woman who was so much in need of being loved, I threw them away. I wanted his love and affection and approval. So we practiced rhythm of a sort, and I fortunately didn't become pregnant for a while.

We got married, and first thing I found out on my wedding day was that the guy I married was on heroin; that he was mainlining, and I didn't know that he was doing drugs before. He had sometimes conned me out of money, but he never ever told me that he was taking heroin. Like he would say he needed the money to go fix my car, and meanwhile he would be buying drugs.

And, you know, he developed this crazy kind of jealousy. He always thought I was looking at his friends, and that I was sneaking around, even though I never had any free time! By this point, I had been with him for two years, and I was—my mind had been twisted by this relationship. I felt desperate, because I had nothing, really, and I had this feeling that, if we were to have a child together, that maybe it would change things. But he wouldn't agree to having a child. So what I did was decide when I was fertile and didn't tell him, and bingo—I got pregnant. Right after that, before I even knew I was pregnant, there was an episode where he beat me up, and I went to my mother's, and he came to my parents' house and threatened my parents. I went to Family Court to get a protection order and he was there and he's yellow as a banana. When I saw the condition he was in, my heart turned, and instead of getting the protection order, I went back with him because the hospital wouldn't take him. In the city at that time, they were getting so many heroin addicts with hepatitis that they would only take the

infectious cases, not these viral cases that were caused by hypo-
dermics. So I went home with him and took care of him.

The first thing he wanted was for me to get an abortion.
Well, I couldn't get an abortion because that guy wasn't on
Rivington Street anymore. It was early 1970, and abortion was
still illegal and there was nothing I could do. Although I might
have been able to go out-of-state to get an abortion, the money
was all gone because he had spent it all on drugs. So there was
no money for an abortion.

Because of the hepatitis, we went on Medicaid, but there was
no funding for abortions then, and I wasn't covered. He was so
unaccepting of this pregnancy that he began accusing me of
getting pregnant with somebody else, and keeping me up all
night trying to get a confession out of me. He would start right
after supper: Whose baby was it, who were you doing it with,
was it this one, was it that one, trying to get a confession out of
me.

Well, as my belly started getting bigger he started getting nut-
sier, and he said, "If you can't get an abortion, I'll give you
one," and he would stand me up against the wall and throw
karate kicks at me and just miss me by a quarter of an inch or
just touch me.

And then, by the time I was five months pregnant, in New
York State you could get an abortion if the pregnancy was a life
hazard or a mental hazard to the mother. Early in pregnancy,
when that torture stuff started, I took fifteen Librium and went
to the hospital, so there was a record in the hospital of a suicide
attempt.

So here I am, five months pregnant and the only way for me
to get an abortion is by working up this thing about the suicide.
At five months pregnant I thought the only way was to do a
Caesarian section, but at that time I was so tormented I was
willing to do anything just to end it. I thought I was going to be
killed or I just wanted to die, and I just didn't care anymore. So
Paul took me into the hospital and I went through this thing
that I'm really suicidal and I just can't take it any longer. They

would have preferred to watch over me and bring the pregnancy to term and give that baby up for adoption, but they refused to do anything unless I was committed. I refused to commit myself voluntarily, but that episode gave Paul the idea of adoption, and even I began thinking about it. I thought, in my heart, I loved the baby inside me and my only option was to give the child up for adoption.

At this point, Paul began to waver: "Oh, I want the baby, oh, I don't want the baby." I was starting to think, I'm going to get away from you, and he would say, "If you try to leave me I'll have you committed and then I'll take that baby and I'll give it to my mother and she'll take care of it." So I thought to myself: "His parents knew he had a drug problem and they used me; 'She's a good little girl, she'll set the boy straight.'" They used me, they were deceitful, they were crazy themselves, and no way would my baby end up with them! If Paul tried to raise the baby, even with me there, there was no way I was going to be able to protect this baby. He was already beating me—what was he going to do to this child? So, I looked through the Yellow Pages and I found the Children's Aid Society, and so one day I went there and I started talking to them, and I started talking to Paul about this agency. I think he came just once, but he couldn't really cope with that—he couldn't cope with anything in life. I was on my own. I couldn't go back to my parents because my father's attitude was, "You made your bed, now lie in it," and also, "Once you leave my home, I'm finished with you; I've done my duty."

So I went to the Children's Aid Society, and there was a woman there who interviewed me many times. In a way it was like therapy for me, because I was able to go to this person alone, and I was able to talk about all these things. And the further along I got in the pregnancy, the more I loved the baby within me, and the more determined that no matter how I felt, I would surrender the child for adoption and tow the line with Paul. I would not give him any reason to renege on the agreement to surrender the child. [Sobbing and holding onto my

hands, she cries for a long time.] God . . . I remember thinking
. . . I'm going to bring this baby into the world and I'm going to
find a decent home for him or her . . . and I did it.

When I went to the hospital there was nobody there that I
knew; I was all alone. I was so depressed, I just wanted to lie
there and I wanted to die. I thought—I can't die, I have to sign
those last papers. What if I don't survive this and Paul changes
his mind, this poor baby is going to be with crazy people for the
rest of his life. God knows what will happen to him. So, I went
through the labor . . . it was a little boy. I had to tell him,
"Maybe you'll understand that I love you so much and that's
why I'm doing this. I'm trying to save your life." At that point,
because of the suicidal stuff, they had a psychiatrist come see
me and they had a birth control lady come to see me. Right
away, the day after delivering the baby, they had a birth control
lady come see me and I had pills before I left the hospital. It's
strange, because he was born in October, and the Children's
Aid Society must have had this thing where they had an interim
period before they would call you back to sign the final, final
papers. At that point, they had adoptive parents. They were able
to tell me that they lived on Long Island and they were finan-
cially stable. So at least I had that comfort.

I grieved and grieved and grieved because of it every October,
for ten years. I would go through this depression that was incredible. I would go through these crying jags and it literally
was not until my second child was born that I wasn't so con-
sumed by grief. So, I went into psychotherapy, with the complete understanding that if I didn't, I might very well repeat this
thing. While I was doing that I started talking about the pregnancy, and the adoption and what went on, and working it out.
Finally I came to the realization that I wasn't a failure because
of what I did. It took a long time—and it's not over.

I'm still waiting for 1988 when I can file my name with that
organization that helps adopted children find their natural parents. Well, as soon as he's eighteen, he is allowed to look for
me, and I'm praying that he will. If abortion had been legal,

and available to me, a poor woman at the time, I would have had an abortion early on. Yes, if abortion had become legal and available I would have done it. I would have felt that I did the best thing possible, but it wasn't available to me. I went through torment. As it turned out, my real need was to meet a man who would let me be me, and have a child. I'm living that now. So the story is winding up with a happy ending. I had a child by my own choice at the time that I decided was right for me. The thing is, what Pat went through, what both of my two sisters went through, it shouldn't be like that—it should be medical. There should be medical assistance in dire circumstances, and dire circumstances is when you decide that you are not prepared to have a child. A woman shouldn't be forced to have children, because maybe a man wants to have the child or maybe the man wants to keep the woman barefoot and pregnant, at home, and his property. If she has enough kids she'll never have enough time to go out and meet people and develop. I want women to be free.

Peter

A tradesman in his mid-thirties, he is soft-spoken, with a bit of a Southern accent.

Everything happened in Florida. I don't really know how to start. I was a kid. I was fifteen. Her parents didn't like me, and it wasn't hard to understand, really, in retrospect, but in those days it was very much the thing, it was a very common concern for parents to be worried about some guy coming along and getting their daughter pregnant and running off—shotgun weddings and that sort of thing. That was the way it was then, it was a different world. Because, you know, for one thing there was no escape. There was no escape from the consequences of an accident, except to involve a great section of your life, presumably the rest of it, when you had to get married. Of course, I cared very much about what happened, but their attitude was more or less from a natural concern, so they hated me, and that made it very difficult for things to work out. They were holding all the cards.

They didn't like me even before she got pregnant because it was evident that we were in love, and we were lovers, you know, fifteen-year-olds can't hide that sort of thing. They don't realize that they're revealing themselves, but they do. And, of course, the only thing they assumed about me was that I had the very worst attitude about it, and it came to work out in just about the very worst way. But there was no alternative.

There was the persecution from all of our peers. They were very hard on anyone who did anything that was outside of very narrow bounds. Very right-wing state. Very narrow. Very hard. Those were the times. They were always ready to persecute anyone then—especially in high school. A bloodless bunch, no heart. There were always some people, fringe people, who weren't like that. But Orlando in the 1960s was like anyplace else in the fifties. It was as backward as Tennessee or Mississippi about those things. The styles came there, as far as fashion, but as far as the fundamental change, it hadn't arrived there at all.

There weren't any sources of information. Well, they came, I believe it was the year after, a year too late. They made some reference to sex education in biology, but what did they really have to say about it? This is the sperm and this is the egg and once a month a woman blah, blah, blah, but it wasn't really practical. It was biology—you dissect a frog this week and they tell you about sex next week. Neither one of them served any purpose whatsoever, except having viewed the frog's intestines. But those were the times. I guess they were even narrower before that, which is hard to imagine.

We used withdrawal, which of course wasn't very successful at all, especially being very young like that. Not very experienced with your body or with your emotions. It was the Gestalt, you see. The whole society was built around: It was good for boys to want to be with girls, but it was bad for girls to want to be with boys, because boys could get girls pregnant and then the girls couldn't have any alternative—there was no birth control, and it was made to be a plaything. It's funny how such a serious thing can be made a toy. It was unreal to everybody that surrounded me. Sexuality and responsibility were completely unreal, so all the things they said about it were completely irrelevant. On the other hand, when it came around to consequences, it was very, very serious. But, of course, there was no way to be prepared for that, unless the parental authority group would counsel you differently—but they told you a lot of crap about everything in those days. It was all bullshit. You know—go to Vietnam and serve your country, and just all that farcical bullshit. For instance, at that time, they would expel you from school if your hair was too long. I was suspended several times for having my hair too long. Three days at a time. Or else, they would tell you not to come back until it was cut. If you didn't come back, the truant officer would come and get you, because it was against the law—so if the principal didn't like your haircut, you could wind up in "kiddy prison" for it. These are the same people who are telling you that you're supposed to be responsible about your sex life. They weren't bad people all of them, I'm thinking of coaches or something like that, you'd have the opportunity to be with a coach and talk informally about that kind of thing. Sometimes, from the very same person's mouth, on the one hand he would say, you're not supposed to do that, and at another time, he would tell you about what a game sex was. He would make a joke or something that would really declare it to be your role as a male to "get" a female without any emotional investment.

My girlfriend was fourteen when the child was born. I was fifteen. She started missing her periods—we knew that much about it—she missed a couple of them, and then it became evident, you could even see that she was getting big.

About the third month she told her parents. Today, if you found out early, you could do something about it. Not only that, but it's just a whole different thing. Today you'd be much less liable to encounter such a stonewall reaction of hatred and wrath from the girl's parents. In particular, if you were willing to try to do something about it. Or if you were not, at least, irresponsible about it. It really wasn't a joke, even though there really wasn't any responsibility I could bear except for guilt. I mean, what could I do? I couldn't give her money. I couldn't marry her. I couldn't do anything, except say good-bye.

Her parents had a traditional, classic response to me. I had done it and gotten away with it, and that was all they knew or ever considered. I was a villain. I was a murderer except she wasn't dead, that's all. It was the only role they could understand for me to play, that I really . . . it never entered their minds that I might have anything to feel about her, any regret about it.

I really feel like it's different today. If it were today, and I knew what the average fifteen-year-old knows today—they know a lot more than I did, they're a lot more socially enlightened and personally enlightened—if the options were open to me, even the very, very worst marriage couldn't have been as bad as losing . . . just good-bye, just good-bye. The very worst couldn't have been as bad as that. Abortion—it's not becoming to speak of abortion about your own living children, but really, if that had been available to her and she had taken that course, she wouldn't have had to go away to a hospital, it probably wouldn't have been publicly known, which it came to be. Not that abortion is an easy way out, but it's easier than something that wasn't her choice. If she could have chosen that path, it probably would have been easier. Undoubtedly easier. There was no option. No option whatsoever. A fifteen-year-old at that time—it was hard enough to know what was going on, much less to try and negotiate the criminal aspect of dealing with something like an abortion. How could a fifteen-year-old move into the crime world and make a deal and be assured of her safety? Her parents in particular were not in favor of that idea at all. I think mine brought it up at the time, but they didn't allow her that option.

She went away. She went away to an unwed mother's home and had the baby. She gave the baby up for adoption. She had to change schools, of course, but it didn't make any difference. It was known. You know, a girl disappears for six months, one of her friends finds out, then they all find out. And then, of course, in those days it was very polarized, the whole thing, you were either very, very bad or very, very good. So, she was made out to be a very bad person, I'm sure about that. She was a good person, so eventually she brought people around, but I'm sure there are people who never forgave her. There was no support for her, or for me, in the community or in the family or anywhere else. Her family took care of her, but basically I'm sure they condemned her.

I saw her only one time after that. I didn't know how I was supposed to feel—I really didn't take this very well, I didn't take it well at all. It's not like I just said good-bye and moved on to my next girlfriend, or something like that. I really was grieving—it really was very hard. When she came back, I couldn't handle my feelings, or the situation, and she couldn't either. We had no knowledge, we didn't know what our emotions were, we didn't know what we should feel, or why, or who was lying, which everybody was. Nobody told us—useful information was not available to us, on an emotional basis or a practical basis, there wasn't anything. Even my peers that knew about it, who wanted to be supportive, had no idea either, so they were supportive by saying things like, "Ha ha ha, you got away with it," which, of course, made me want to puke.

My parents basically did nothing. What could they do? They worked out a financial sharing of the expenses of sending her to the home, but outside of that, their attitude was very much like the public, that I'd gotten out of it lightly, and I should forget about it. Weird, huh? Weird parents. . . .

I had traveled, I had been in a military family, and it wasn't hard for me to entertain questions that other people didn't entertain. All these things that I'm talking about, I pondered over them a lot, thought about them a great deal. I still don't have my answers, but I did think about them a lot. Without any humility at all, I was ahead of my time, at that place in that time. I'm sure that there are other men, boys, who would have felt very responsible about it, but there was no way to talk about it. The only thing they would tell you in school . . . They told you so much bullshit. They had a counselor in that high school, God, was she a horrible woman. She had no idea about anything. She was narrow, personally bigoted. I don't know how she got in her position. I doubt if she had very much psychological qualification at all.

This situation was very, very bad. I left high school. School wasn't going that great for me anyway, but after this, it got much, much worse. This was the end of my childhood, that's for sure. It was also the end of my school years, although I was forced to be in school for a while after that. I was emotionally destroyed. I was. What I say to myself to describe how I felt then, in a few words: I was fifteen when she went away to have the baby, I bowed my head, and I didn't raise it back up until I was at least nineteen or twenty. It was very, very hard for me . . . the guilt. Because I loved her, but there was nothing to do, nothing to be done, nothing to know. So that was that. So then when she came back, it was quite impossible. I couldn't handle myself, she couldn't handle herself. Her parents couldn't handle her or me or themselves. I couldn't handle her parents or my parents. I'm not joking when I say five years, I bowed my head for five years, because I did.

LEAVING THE COUNTRY

Emily

Emily is a self-made woman. She has been on her own since she was fifteen. "I had plans," she says, "Even as an adolescent I was a person of determination. I thought I was going to lead a very glamorous life and become very successful and show everybody. And I did . . . I have . . . I am."

In 1955, the end of 1955, I was living in Philadelphia, alone in a basement apartment. I was working part time in Horn & Hardart's to support myself. I was going to high school at night to get a diploma to qualify for college. I was, I guess, twenty.

I was having a relationship with a young man, my first actual experience with a man, and I found myself pregnant. I found it unbelievable! I knew that I could not bring a child . . . I could not take care of a child. I knew that I was frightened and alone and impoverished. I had dreams about my life, so there was absolutely no way that I would give up what I was going to become. I didn't want a child. I didn't feel I could take care of a child. I was a baby myself.

I've always been alone. I've been alone since I was sixteen, so it was very bad. I didn't feel like I could tell friends. I didn't have those kind of friends. I wouldn't tell my Philadelphia friends because they would consider it shameful.

At that time it was impossible to get an abortion in Philadelphia because there had been a recent tragedy. The daughter of an upper-middle-class family who owned a chain of supermarkets—I think they were called Food Fair—had just died on an abortionist's table. Everyone was terrified. There was absolutely nothing to be done. Imagine how terrified I felt. Anyway, I went to New York looking for an abortionist. I didn't know anybody and I talked to a lot of people. I sat on park benches . . . absolutely terrified . . . I just didn't know what to do. I got the name of a doctor on Park Avenue and, mind you, I didn't have any money, but I thought I could surely borrow money from somewhere. Oh, yes, I borrowed the money from the man I used to work for in Philadelphia. I told him that I was ill and I had no money and no insurance. I didn't have my family, and I wouldn't have told them anyway because they're not the kind of family you could discuss such things with.

So I went to this Park Avenue doctor, who was absolutely adamant that he did not give abortions. He said that he thought that I ought to have the child and, "How did I get myself into such a situation?" And then there was a doctor down on the Lower East Side that I went to see. He looked to me to be very sinister. There was an unhealthy, unclean air about that place, and I was frightened. Anyway, I happened to bump into someone on the street that I had gone to high school with in Philadelphia. She was an airline stewardess, and I thought ah ha, she must have some experience because she had had such a bad rep in school. So I asked her if she knew of an abortionist, not for me, of course, but for my friend. "No," she said, but she had a friend who was going to Cuba to have an abortion, and maybe my friend wanted to go with her friend. So I asked for her number and I called her. She was married to a Cuban and she was going to stay with his family. She was destitute and she said if I paid her way down and back, and paid for her abortion (which only cost thirty-five dollars) that I could go with her and stay with her family. So I did.

And she was very kind to me. I went to the abortionist with her . . . she had hers first and I heard her screaming and I was absolutely terrified. I said I simply did not want to go through that without some medication and sodium pentothal. And they did give it to me. I was sure that I was never going to wake up again. When it was over I went and stayed with these people for a while, and then I came back to America resolved that I would never sleep with another man again. It had been such an awful experience. Mind you, prior to trying to find an abortionist I had done all these other things. Whatever the remedies were at the time, whatever they were, I tried everything. Like someone told me about drinking a glass of hot gin.

Well, six months later I found myself in the very same predicament, even though I had used a diaphragm. I was stunned by this. I went to Cuba again. I knew where those people lived, and I didn't call or write to them first. I just showed up at their door and asked them if I could stay with them again and they said yes, and I went back to the very same abortionist. This time she said that there were problems and she couldn't do it. So then I had to go and find somebody else and once again it was more asking around. I told the family I was staying with what was wrong and they put me on to other people and there was a series of knocking on doors, asking. It was the beginning of the crackdown in Cuba . . . It was the beginning of the Castro movement and everybody was feeling very threatened. I met a German refugee in a little hotel. He suggested that I move into that hotel and said he would fix me up with an abortionist that he knew—a Frenchwoman. I moved into this hotel and the man attempted to rape me . . . But I did go to the abortionist that he had suggested, and I did get the abortion. This is a story I tell nobody. It's so dreadful an experience.

Anyway, I met some students in Cuba and I stayed for three months. When I came back to New York I got a job as a secretary. I never became pregnant again until I was married and had my three children on the rhythm system, all planned and that was it.

You know, I am plagued by my childhood . . . plagued by it. And here I am fifty years old and I can still tell you what my mother never did for me. I grew up in Philadelphia and my mother left me at the age of sixteen. She felt that she had come to America at thirteen without the language and she was illiterate. I could read, write, and speak the language and she thought I ought to be on my own. She'd had enough. She had a very hard life. She raised five children working day and night in a grocery store in her cellar. We were not your typical Jewish family. None of my sisters, nobody in my family graduated from high school.

My mother went to Atlantic City, can you believe it? She bought a big old rooming house on St. Charles Place in Atlantic City and she rented rooms. It makes me laugh every time I play Monopoly. My mother was . . . is an admirable woman as far as I'm concerned, despite her treatment of me. She's still alive, in her nineties. She came to America on her own at thirteen. She worked as a maid in somebody's house. It's not as if she had some easy life. She was an embittered woman who had struggled to raise her children. When my mother went to Atlantic City, my father went to live with his cronies in west Philadelphia. They were socialists and a bunch of men that I absolutely had no patience with. He certainly offered to take me, but I was already a snob at that age. The men were beneath me and I didn't want to associate with them. They were a very grimy group and it was a very filthy house, so I went off on my own.

They were not a family with great aspirations and expectations. But I had them. Probably from watching a lot of movies . . . and reading a lot of rags-to-riches stories. As a matter of fact I was going to be a movie star, but now I think, ironically, I have a daughter who's a movie star. It amuses me. Even as an adolescent I was a person of determination. My motivation was strongly rooted, and it's still there. At a very early age I had plans. I thought I was going to lead a very glamorous life and become very successful and show everybody. And I did . . . I have . . . I am. I published fiction, I was an editor at a publishing house, and I had owned an art gallery that was very successful. I was successful, as I am today. I never finished high school, but I went to Columbia in 1970 on every scholarship and fellowship and thing available. But I had already become successful, so it wasn't as if they were betting on some unknown. And none of it could have happened if I had a child. Of course not. Back then I could hardly support myself.

There was no conflict about it. I absolutely did not want a child. I don't weep for it, I don't pine for it, I think I did the right thing. I did want to have a family eventually, and my kids are real important to me. But raising those three kids, I always think, my God, you made the right decision. I could not imagine what my life would have been like had I had those children, except it would have been impoverished.

I have very strong feelings about adolescents having babies. Very negative feelings. Those children come into this world without asking for it. They deserve to be coddled, to be given some advantages, some things. A child of fifteen or sixteen is just a baby herself. There's no way that a person of sixteen or seventeen can raise a child with any intelligence. I really don't think so. And I think that we're all so frail and our early lives really set us up forever and I cannot believe that a sixteen- or seventeen-year-old child knows how to raise a child . . . I think babies deserve better. I don't have feelings of admiration for these young kids who decide to keep their babies, I really don't. They can only raise miserable children, and I feel bad about that. They can have an abortion now without the pain and fear that I had.

I was very active in the Women's Movement early on, and I have been very active in the abortion movement. At Columbia I went on all those marches and demonstrations and signed those petitions. Those years are so vivid to me that seeing these kids who are uninvolved in the issue . . . abortion has always been there for them. They don't know what it was like before, and what it might be like if it's taken away. They just don't know what it was like.

Jenny

The first thing that strikes you about Jenny is her thick, shoulder-length white-blond hair. There is a pale, ethereal quality to her prettiness: At forty-four, she still has the aura of a flower child of the sixties.

In the cafeteria where she suggested we meet, Jenny puts her feet up, makes herself comfortable, and begins talking without regard for being overheard. She punctuates her wry humor with laughter as she talks, letting you in on the joke, making you want to laugh with her.

When you wanted to find an abortionist, it wasn't like you could call your friendly neighborhood clinic. It wasn't like it was a widely known phone number. You had to start with whoever you thought might have had one.

The first abortion I had was in 1960 in Seattle. I was not married to the father. No, no I wasn't. I was seeing him and he moved to New York to go to Cooper Union, so I borrowed money from my brother. My brother asked me if I would prefer to get married. I guess he was going to use a shotgun on Dave, and, uh, I thought that was really sweet of him and very supportive. I guess he thought that was the right thing to do.

I certainly did not feel that I was about to marry Dave. He's still a dear friend of mine, and I adore him now as I did then, but I no more feature him as a life companion and husband now than I did then. I featured him as a boyfriend. I did not feel that it was going to last. I was far too young for that kind of thing.

Dave knew about it, but he felt like I was taking care of it. I didn't make a big fuss about it. I was a year older than he was, and, uh, he was what, nineteen, twenty, and he just really did not have any big ideas on the subject, as long as I wasn't upset. And I wasn't. It really didn't even occur to me not to have an abortion, so the problem was to find an abortionist, and that was easy enough, because everybody I knew had seemed to. They all chose abortions. I never seriously considered giving it up for adoption. I did not fancy going through a nine-month, you know, losing nine months of my life. I had fancy plans. It was a sort of déclassé thing to do, have a baby and give it up for adoption.

I don't remember having any difficulty finding an abortionist. I know it was in the same building as my friend Ann's abortionist, so maybe I got the name from her. Everybody I knew at college probably used an abortionist at that Schaeffer Building. I took a bus to Seattle and stayed with friends there.

By that time I was real close to three months pregnant, right at the three-month mark, so I was uncomfortable about that. I remember thinking at the last minute that maybe he wouldn't do it. And a little uncomfortable about the whole sequence of events: of showing up there—was he really going to be there, and what did I do at this point if he wasn't? Was the money going to be sufficient? And also I was worried about what if it were twins, because I was already beginning to get a fair amount of stomach. [Laughing] I wondered if he would charge more.

I don't remember checking his wall for pieces of paper, but I'm quite sure he was a doctor. He did an ordinary D&C. He used gas. The one weird note was that I felt him massaging my vulva, waiting for me to go out under the gas. It went on for an exceptionally long time, but I was afraid if I said anything he might tell me to get up off the table. The only patient-teaching he did was what to do: something along the lines of "Don't call us . . . ."

I don't know why I didn't go back up to Seattle for the second abortion. I'm sure I must have considered it, so maybe they were no longer in business. I was still living in San Francisco, but for that one I asked around. I asked a neighbor and said, "I have a friend. . . ." And she said, "Why doesn't your friend ask her doctor?" Oh, she really didn't want to hear this.

It was a couple of years later. The way I got pregnant was that I stopped using birth control so that I could have a baby 'cause my husband was about to be snatched into the Army. However, the Army did not take him because they immediately took one look at him and gave him a 2Y. That's what they do if you're crazy, you know. He started to act crazy and even before he could say, "I'm crazy," they said, "You're crazy," and they sent him right out. He was actually a little disappointed that he didn't get to finish his schpiel. He has since completely disappeared. Anyway, he was in favor of my having a baby. He thought we were in a terrific situation to have a baby. He didn't have a job, I was supporting him, he was drinking and carrying on with his buddies. He was crazy. Finally I said to myself, "Gee, I don't think this is the right situation for me," and left him. When I discovered I was pregnant, I immediately opted to look around for an abortionist. When my husband found out through channels that I was pregnant, he was infuriated that I was not keeping the baby because it was half his baby. I didn't need this kind of consciousness-raising. So I borrowed three hundred dollars from my friend Cynthia—you always go to your friends—and got the name of a Mexican abortionist in Juarez from Molly. Molly was a college friend who had had five abortions, so she was the expert. I said, "Molly, about this . . ." And she said, "Here, here's a name." Molly subsequently died under an avalanche. After five abortions, to have an avalanche squish you to death is a weird fate. Anyway, I never could understand why she had five abortions, but even that I considered a better way of operating than to have babies and give them up for adoption.

Anyway, you called up this number in Mexico and made an

appointment, and then you flew to Juarez. I flew by myself, because I could not afford two plane tickets.

Anyway, I took a cab from the El Paso airport to the abortionist's address. They were very cheerful there. It was a suburban Mexican house, pink wrought iron, stucco, tiled, and clean. A lot of people were there, a lot of women. Kind of an "up" atmosphere. It was a mother and son team. The mother did the abortion and the son assisted her. These guys seemed quite capable. Raoul leaned on my knee while his mother peered down my vagina and checked out my cervix. They were a great team. I loved their act. The son was the nurse, but they made no pretense at being a real doctor and nurse. I had no idea what their medical training was. Because this was Mexico, and she was an older woman, I assumed she had not been to medical school. You came into the waiting room, and there were several people waiting, some of them in couples, others by themselves. I was nervous. I was thinking, "If I start to hemorrhage here, how the hell am I going to get back to the United States to go to a hospital?" I worried about infection, and I just hoped they sterilized their instruments. But there would be enough time to worry about an infection if I got an infection. My worry about hemorrhaging was more immediate, because I did not know how I would get to a hospital and I wasn't sure that they would assist me. I wasn't sure how safe the situation really was. I wasn't sure what they would do with hemorrhaging. I hoped they just avoided that situation.

So they took me into a room with an examining table with stirrups, and they dilated my cervix without any anesthesia. That was painful. I don't know why they did it without anesthesia, because after that they gave me sodium pentothal. Yes, yes I'm sure that's what it was. So I don't remember anything about the procedure itself. But I assume it was a D&C. That's how it seemed. I woke up in a little bedroom with two beds in it and little magazine pictures of six-year-old brides on the walls. They were little girls wearing confirmation dresses. There was a woman lying in the next bed.

This was not a stay-here-twelve-hours-operation, but they did keep you until they thought you could walk safely. I wasn't hemorrhaging when I left.

I remember I was still feeling the aftereffects of the drug. I was in a wonderful frame of mind, very cheerful and happy because of the sodium pentothal, so I kind of floated out the door saying, "Thank you very much. Had a delightful time." And into a cab which swept me back to the airport. I flew back to San Francisco. I didn't hemorrhage, and I didn't get an infection, and I was just very thankful that I got away with it. I mean, I didn't know anybody who died having an abortion, but I knew that it was a real possibility. It was a great relief not being pregnant anymore.

Sex in the early sixties when I went to college in Berkeley was not only okay, it was like a badge of seniority. The big kids did it. It was proof that you were a young liberated person. Abortion was an offshoot of that. But abortion was always an item of gossip. I'm not really big on being gossiped about, so I only discussed it with people I discussed other intimate details of my life with. I did not discuss it with men because they didn't know anything about it. They couldn't really empathize. All they could contribute to the discussion was, "Oh, my girlfriend asked me for money." Nobody ever really called them in on much more at the time except for guilt and money. And probably not in that order.

Melissa

She describes herself, at nineteen, as the quintessential unfit mother: unstable, confused, and rebellious. She seems to raise the question herself: "Would you have wanted this irresponsible girl to be responsible for raising a child?"

Years have passed, and with effort and purpose she has changed dramatically.

She is now the loving and devoted mother of a four-year-old girl. "I feel sorry for those kids who are dying all their lives because they were born. I didn't want my child to suffer because I wouldn't have been a good mother at that time. I was too young and involved with myself. I guess inside I knew someday I'd grow up and then I'd be ready. And that's what happened."

The first time, it must have been the late sixties—1967. I was about to graduate high school, and I was pregnant and had planned to have an abortion. But two days before, I had a miscarriage. At that time, my boyfriend planned the abortion and I felt I just had to do it. I was not capable of taking care of a kid and I knew that I wanted to do other things. I didn't know what with, but I knew that I didn't want to be trapped with a baby and I knew that my father would kill me. And I just couldn't face hurting them—my parents. I think that the idea was that I didn't want my father to imagine me having sex. I was embarrassed about it, for him to think that I was doing that.

So I would always lie and lie and lie. Ultimately, I stayed alone in my room for twelve hours in labor having a miscarriage. Finally, I couldn't stand it anymore, and we went to Montefiore Hospital, and I was in the hospital for four days. They had to do a D&C and everything. And my father had to sign the form so I could get morphine because I was in such pain. So he found out, and he had been strict anyway, but now he was even stricter. And, the next time I got pregnant was not long after that.

At the time I was working and living with my boss, who was an older woman with a family. She was divorced. I felt I was— she was taking care of me and the abortion. This woman I lived with wasn't my mother, but she was like a parent figure and I guess she had a sense of, "Oh, I don't want this to happen. She's too young to have to deal with having a child without having a husband, and without anybody with her." I really didn't have that much to do with it. The plane reservations were made to Puerto Rico. It was illegal then, but I wasn't worried because these older people were taking care of me. This woman arranged it and went with me to Puerto Rico. She knew the doctor and we went into this hospital for pregnant women where he did abortions on the side. That part of it was a very bad experience. I don't know what they did—I woke up and there was a lot of blood all over. I felt very alone and wasted. I felt sorry for myself. I was young, I was very young, and I felt sorry for myself. Like I was a victim. And yet it was my doing too. I could have taken precautions and I didn't. I don't know what the root of that is, but I never took precautions.

Another time I went to Puerto Rico with my mother. I was pregnant and she took me there. We were in a doctor's office and they didn't give me anything and I wasn't allowed to scream. It was very painful. Again, I felt like I was being moved around.

This was in the late sixties. Sex was going on. I was young— everything was a big party. I wasn't thinking about anything. It was what was going on at that time. Everybody was having sex with everyone. A couple of the would-be fathers were pretty heavy relationships, but I never considered staying with them. I wasn't really thinking about the future.

Birth control to me was a turnoff. I had a diaphragm and I didn't use it. It bothered me. Condoms—I would rather not have sex. I couldn't take birth control pills because I had a damaged liver. So, it was like tempting fate—it was like a gamble. I knew I was tempting fate and then after I was pregnant, it was taken care of. I don't know if I was rebelling against my strict father—there must be some reason I was chronically pregnant. I knew it would be taken care of. Maybe it was the attention I was getting when I was pregnant, you know, that these older people, these parent figures, were paying attention to me. They were taking care of me, because I was in a position where I couldn't do it myself. Because when it was illegal, I couldn't go and get an abortion, so somebody—in these times when it was illegal, you really had to have a connection for an abortion in Puerto Rico. It was always done by these people who had connections. Maybe that was it.

I had an abortion with the father of my child now. I had an abortion while I was with him earlier in our relationship. I didn't have the feeling that I wanted to have the baby. I always justified it that I loved my child too much to have it. A child suffers when it's alive, not when it's not formed yet. I feel strongly, and that's why abortions were nothing to me. I never felt guilty. It was painful, especially the ones in Puerto Rico— the bad experiences I had in Puerto Rico . . . where one time my mother went. I was under the sodium pentothal and I thought I was dead and they were trying to wake me up. I couldn't respond so I thought, "They don't know that I'm not dead," and I remember screaming for my mother, and she came to the recovery room. That was a very horrible experience, but it wasn't horrible enough for me not to do it again.

It was, I guess, a form of birth control. It's true: If I get pregnant, I'll just have an abortion. It was expensive, but I wasn't paying for it, my father was. But I'd pay him back. I was work-

ing, so I paid him twenty-five dollars a week and eventually he'd
be paid back. It was also the sense of being moved around, you
know, "I'm pregnant—take care of me." I could have avoided
it, but I did get pregnant: "Here I am pregnant now—helpless."
That kind of a feeling. Now everyone around me, they're making the phone calls, they're making the arrangements and I walk
in and fifteen minutes later I'm not pregnant anymore. I never
put any kind of thing on the guys. It never was, "You got me
pregnant, now you owe me something." It wasn't that at all. I
never wanted to be tied down to someone, so it wasn't that.

It wouldn't be as easy emotionally to have an abortion now
after having my child. But it was different then. I'm glad I did
have the abortions that I had. I'm glad that I didn't have a child
in those days. I think that what I did was right. Now I consider
myself a really good mother because I wanted this child. Before,
I wasn't ready and it wasn't fair to the child. That was very
important during the abortion years. I just didn't see myself as a
mother. I couldn't relate to it at all. I hated the people who
were against abortion. I hated them. It was like they were sen-
tencing women. To me, having a child at that point would have
been a jail sentence. A very foreboding thought—to be
trapped—to be held down for so many years. It was unthinkable
that people were forced to do that. Or being jeopardized by
having illegal abortions that were very, very dangerous, with
coat hangers or whatever.

I do remember where I worked, there was a very, very, very
rich girl, WASP, very proper family. She got pregnant and she
came to me to ask if I would arrange it for her and pick her up
after the abortion. Nobody knew except me. I mean, this was
the kind of person who wouldn't give me the time of day, but
she knew that if anybody could do this it would be me, because
of my views. Her views were completely different. This is the
hypocrisy; she would put down abortion with her peers. But yet
she had an abortion.

Ann

On March 9, 1986, Ann, her grown daughter and niece traveled together by bus to Washington, D.C., to demonstrate for abortion rights. Although it has been the motivating force behind her activism, until now Ann has never revealed what she tells here.

I had two illegal abortions. The first was in 1956 when I was twenty-five. I had lived with my husband for about two years before we went to Europe, and we got married because we wanted to go to Europe. In those days it was not common for unmarried people to travel together. I had gotten pregnant after we were married just a few months, while we were in Europe. I think of it as my "European Odyssey: Looking for an Abortion." My husband wasn't opposed to keeping the child, but you know who the burden would have fallen on. It would have changed my life more than his.

It caused a lot of tension between us, but I knew that I didn't want to have a child. I wasn't a feminist then. I didn't know about it, but I did know that I only wanted to have a child when I wanted to have a child, and I did not want to have *this* child. It seemed very elementary to me. I don't remember when it was that I learned I was pregnant. It was probably in Spain. We were visiting friends in Spain, who were actually Dutch, who had a Dutch friend in Paris, but I don't remember going directly to Paris. I remember getting some pills in Austria. Probably something that contained ergot. I had cramps, but it didn't work. So we went to Germany to some friends of my husband—a childless couple who said they would adopt the child if we wanted, but I really didn't want to go through that.

I don't know how, but then we found out about a place in Germany. It was a maternity hospital. We had to give the doctor three hundred dollars in cash, which in those days was a lot of money. He pretended I was bleeding, and told the nurse it was an emergency and performed a D&C. I really got quite good care. I was in the hospital for five days and was treated quite well. It was just that: three hundred dollars not to have a child.

I don't remember being emotionally involved in it at all. All my feelings were cut off. It was something I just needed to do, and I did it.

Then, when we got back to New York, about two or three years later I got pregnant again. I had known about Dr. Spencer, but he was no longer performing abortions at that time, so I found out through a friend about a doctor in West New York, New Jersey. It took some time to find him. It was hard at that time to find someone who would perform an abortion. It was all very secretive, like they had a code name "Charlie," and you had to call at a certain time on a certain day, and I think you had to use a code name too. It was really bizarre that in New York it was more difficult to find somebody than it was in Europe. I remember someone told me that if you'd take lots of hot baths that would cause an abortion, and where we were living we didn't have a bathtub, so I went to visit my sister upstate. It was hot baths and mustard, I think. I didn't even tell her that was what I was trying to do, but I arranged to take as many hot baths over the weekend as I could, but it didn't help.

I remember going to this doctor's office on a Saturday, and the office was empty and he didn't use any anesthesia. It was very painful, but in a way I was lucky because the woman who told me about him had to have an abortion a few months later, and she had all kinds of terrible complications from it. Evidently she had two embryos, and the doctor only found one of them, and she developed septicemia and was very ill. So, even though I had two abortions I think I was really lucky, not having any side effects. It sounds really simple now, but it was not simple. It was like I wasn't being allowed to decide my own future, and that seemed very important to me; that I could decide when I wanted to have a child. Nobody knew. A few friends, but I don't think I even told my sister. I don't think it was an experience that I shared with many friends. Until I met you on the bus the other day, I hadn't even told my kids.

It was something that each of us tried to put aside. The woman I met for a drink this evening before I came here said, "There were so many of us who had to do that." Until today I never knew that she had had an abortion. It was a part of hidden history.

At the time, I didn't let myself think or feel. It was just something I needed to do, and I did whatever I needed to do to get it accomplished. I just didn't want to have a child then, and I'm glad I didn't, because it would have meant bringing a child I resented into this world. Once I decided it was time, it was easy. I had one child, and then I decided to have another one and I did. My son Peter is twenty-three, and my daughter is now twenty-one.

It's funny, now that I talk about it, I feel no emotion at all. It's like I was twenty-five again and going through that experience. [She looks pained, hugs herself around her abdomen.] I just feel tight in my gut. I'm not relating to it emotionally at all . . . and that's what I did then. I just did what I had to do. That was my mechanism for dealing with those things.

Talking about it now is reliving . . . it's reliving those days, which were painful in a lot of ways . . . My way of dealing with things in those days was not to talk about it. . . . [Close to tears, her voice becomes very quiet.] This is the first time I've talked about this in a very long time. It was sad that we had to go through that.

It was a waste. A waste of people's time and money and energy. I feel I was lucky, given the things that happened to me. I knew kids that I went to junior high with who suddenly were no longer in junior high, and you'd see them out later with a baby carriage, and friends of mine who had to get married while they were in college because they were pregnant. So I think I was lucky. It was costly, but I still managed to survive it and not have to have a child when I didn't want it, until I was ready.

I didn't have any conscious feelings about being a feminist, but I certainly knew that I wanted to be able to determine my life. Of course, once I had children, my life changed in all the ways I didn't want it to change [chuckle], but of course I didn't know that then.

Later, my sister needed to have an abortion, and it was easier for me to ask for help for her. It was so difficult for me, turning myself over to other people who would determine what would happen to me.

It's strange, now that I'm talking about this I feel cold . . . I feel so cold . . .

" YOU MADE YOUR BED , NOW LIE IN IT . "

Sometimes when you have scrutinized a face long and persistently, you seem to discover a second face hidden behind the one you see. This is generally an unmistakable sign that this soul harbors an emigrant who has withdrawn from the world in order to watch over secret treasure, and the path for the investigator is indicated by the fact that one face lies beneath the other, as it were, from which he understands that he must attempt to penetrate within if he wishes to discover anything. The face, which ordinarily is the mirror of the soul, here takes on, though it be but for an instant, an ambiguity that resists artistic production. An exceptional eye is needed to see it . . . to follow this infallible index of secret grief.

—Søren Kierkegaard,
Either/Or

Liz

She teaches Contemporary Literature at a large Midwestern university. "It took me so long to get my Ph.D. that by the time I finished, the literature almost wasn't contemporary anymore."

During the long afternoon that we spent in her sunroom, Liz speaks thoughtfully, measuring what she says, pausing between sentences to get a sense of where she's going next.

She had the prototypical shotgun wedding. "The children don't know that I was pregnant when I married their father, but now I really want to tell them, to give them a different way of understanding me and our family's history. I was so ashamed for so many years that I never talked about this. I thought what I had done was utterly disgraceful. It's a great relief to talk about it, now that I have forgiven myself for being human."

You don't even hear about shotgun weddings anymore. Nobody has to get married these days. Remember how many jokes there used to be about shotgun weddings? I suppose people made jokes about it because it was too painful to talk about directly. Even now it's really hard for me to explain how something like that could have happened to me. Since I first talked with you, I've thought a lot about my story, about what I would want to tell you, but it's difficult because there was no convenient beginning, middle and end. It went on for years, and some of the

things that happened to me may be relevant to your interests
and maybe some are not. I'll just tell you how it happened.

Things were so different then, in the late fifties, before the
Women's Movement changed the way we think about women
and what they should do with their lives. It seemed to me,
when I was a teenager, that everyone wanted me to be something I wasn't, and no one had the slightest inkling of what I
was, including me. The people closest to me, my parents, their
friends, family, all the adults around me seemed to confirm one
thing: I was a good student who worked hard and got A's in
school. Except for that, they seemed to be constantly horrified
by the "radical" things I said, and they generally responded to
me as if there were great cause for concern about the way my
brain worked, or didn't work. Mostly, I just wanted to be a
beatnik.

When I was nineteen, in my sophomore year of college, I
was going out with a boy I had met that summer in my hometown in Wisconsin. We had both gone East—he went to work,
I went to college—so we continued seeing each other every
weekend. It was a very confusing time for me. I was trying to
deal with being physically attracted to him and not wanting to
be a "bad girl," or ruin my reputation. Those days, sex was
everywhere, but not openly as it is now. No explicit movies or
sex manuals or songs. It was sort of hidden behind a guise of
innocence. Imagine: Marilyn Monroe was the national heroine,
the ultimate sex symbol, and girls everywhere were supposed to
dress up in strapless dresses and four-inch heels, but we weren't
supposed to have sex. We were supposed to have love and romance.

It was doubly confusing to me, because I had been encouraged by my mother to dress and look very attractive and seductive. I was attractive to men, but I was not supposed to be
attracted to them. My total sex education from her was "Keep
them at an arm's length." All this was complicated by the fact
that my father died when I was seventeen, and I was pretty
desperate for attention from a man.

Anyway, I was in a fog in those days about what to do with myself. Being away from home had been quite an experience, but the idea of choosing a career—or even choosing a college major—had some pretty heady implications, and I didn't even know how to begin thinking about those things, so I concentrated on being swept off my feet instead. A lot of other women seemed to be doing the same thing.

So, that second year at college—it was a small women's college—I had convinced my mother to give me "blanket per," which meant permission to leave the campus for the weekend. Can you believe it? In those days we had to sign out and give an address, a girlfriend's of course, so I'd put down some friend's number and end up at my boyfriend's apartment.

The man I was dating was living in Boston, working at his first job. He had a career! It seemed very grown-up, visiting him on weekends. We would make candlelight dinners and be very romantic, and during Christmas vacation we met each other's friends and family back home. We knew a lot of the same people, but we had not met before because he had already graduated from high school when I was just starting. I had heard of him, though, and a few people who knew him had warned me not to get involved with him. His friends nicknamed him "Grumpy," and they used to joke with me about "How can you put up with him?" At the time, I just thought they were being funny. He was so handsome and sort of brash—it seemed like self-confidence to me. It wasn't until much later that I figured out that arrogance is not the same thing as confidence.

When we saw each other it was easy to be on our best behavior. We were always doing something interesting and getting dressed up, going places, and it was usually only one or two nights a week.

Eventually we tried experimenting with sex, in a sort of furtive, incomplete way. It wasn't as if we planned ahead and really enjoyed it. At least I didn't. I always felt guilty and scared. I don't know what he felt, but then our sex life was always like that, disconnected. Once I had gotten an IUD, after my third child, and I was no longer afraid of getting pregnant, I realized that he was the one who actually had serious sexual problems under all that bravado.

Anyway, this one weekend I had just had my period and I guess I was feeling daring, so we "went all the way" and I got pregnant. I can't even begin to tell you what a nightmare that was. I was frantic, and I felt like I was drowning, I was so scared.

My best friend went with me to a doctor in a little town where no one would know me. We went to this doctor we found in the Yellow Pages to find out if I was pregnant. Ann waited for me and I went into his dingy office alone. I pretended to be secretly married, but he obviously didn't believe my story. He was asking all kinds of questions about my circumstances. He spent a lot more time examining me than I thought was necessary. He took his time and spoke to me in this unctuous, patronizing way. It's horrifying, now that I know what a gynecologist is supposed to do. Aagh, it gives me the creeps . . . he was so sleazy! You know, now that we're talking about this— I'll bet this man was an abortionist! He was asking all kinds of questions about my circumstances. At the time, I just thought he was a pervert. I'd never seen a sleazy doctor before. I swear I remember him with dirty fingernails.

I went back to the dorm and cried and cried. I took scalding hot baths for days and tried to throw myself down the stairs—I'd heard that was the way women had miscarriages—but that was difficult to do without hurting myself. It was April, and before I got pregnant I had been accepted as a transfer student to the University of Michigan. I really wanted to go there to study journalism. The idea of going to an enormous school like that with a well-known faculty seemed like the big time to me. When I was thinking about it I remember Bruce used to say things like, "You'll go off and marry some lawyer and I'll never see you again." I remember sort of halfheartedly reassuring him that I'd wait, but I really knew that two years at a big university would put a lot of distance between us. I didn't allow myself to think about that once I found out I was pregnant.

I told him I was definitely pregnant, and it was just sort of assumed that we'd get married, and I thought that was my punishment for being involved in sex. So I just accepted it. I didn't think about getting an abortion, because all I knew about it was that that's where you went to be killed. There had been articles in the local paper about women being mutilated and abortionists being arrested. I'm sure if anyone I trusted had tried to help me get one, or had known anything about it, I would have. No one did. But even if I'd had connections, I would have been terrified. To die that way, on an abortionist's table, would have been the ultimate disgrace: everyone would have known I was pregnant! But if it had been safe, I would have done it. No question.

I never told anyone at school except Ann. I was much too ashamed. I managed to get through my final exams, and then I went home to break the news. I was in the kitchen, and I remember blurting out the line I had rehearsed to tell my mother. "Mother, I'm pregnant and Bruce and I are getting married." She screamed for my older brother and then fainted, right there in the kitchen! That was the only time I ever saw her do that! When I tried to talk to her, she said something about how I had ruined her life, and how could I do this to her. Then she went to bed and stayed there until the wedding. She must have managed to use the phone, though, because two of her friends came over and asked me very pointedly about whether I really loved him. Everyone seemed to ask the same question. "Do you love him?" What was I going to say? "No, I'm just a tramp"?

One of the women who came over to talk to me was actually a nice lady who probably really cared about me. Do you know, it was only after I talked to you about your project that it hit me—twenty-six years later—that what she really might have been asking me was whether I wanted out. But I couldn't see or hear. All I knew was that I had to get married to make it right, and then I would escape from this terrible shame and go far away and start a new life, and no one would ever know.

Of course, I had convinced myself that what I wanted most in life was to marry this guy and have this child, and the whole atmosphere at the time made it impossible for me to do anything else. I was so ashamed. So, rather than admit any doubts, I denied the whole thing. My mother's reaction was, "You made your bed, now lie in it." So I did. I talked to Bruce's mother and his family made the arrangements. His mother was very nice to me, actually.

I was a basket case, but I was trying to make it look as if I knew what I was doing.

We got married right away. Bruce flew home that weekend for the wedding. We were married in the Methodist Church. The ceremony is a big blur to me, except I remember feeling terrified. I can still see myself kneeling there at the altar, crying. I guess it must have passed for tears of joy.

I went back to Boston with him and we got an apartment and settled into being married. We fought about everything. He criticized everything I did. I spent a lot of time on the roof, crying. I was always exhausted, working full time in the heat, and pregnant. And he blamed me for not being able to whiz through the housework on Saturday and Sunday. At the same time, he was always bragging about me to his friends and he loved to show me off in public. He brought home dinner guests all the time, and I got very good at turning out candlelight dinners. He loved playing "Happy Family," and he loved the part I played in it too: I was his number-one prop.

Once the baby came and I took him home with me, I was absolutely captivated. He was adorable and very good-natured, the best company I'd ever had. I took him everywhere with me, shopping, museums, lunch with friends. He was a delight, but nothing could have smoothed out the relationship I had with his father. I was using birth control—I had a diaphragm—but it didn't work. I had hardly recovered and gotten back on my feet when I was pregnant again. The second child was premature, and I'd had a really hard time while I was pregnant. He was born seven weeks early, about big enough to hold in one hand. He had to stay, swaddled up tight, all alone in the hospital nursery for a month. They never let me hold him or feed him. I looked through the glass window at him, and then I went home crying. By the time he came home, he was still scrawny, barely five pounds, needing to be fed every two or three hours. I was devastated. I couldn't seem to feel anything but exhaustion. It wasn't that I didn't want him, it was just that I didn't want to have all these children. I was only twenty-one, unhappy, and I had to give up going to school again to take care of this tiny, helpless infant. I had been having a pretty good time with the first one, but two in diapers was pretty overwhelming. My husband never once got up during the night and never changed a diaper or fed them. I was depressed and wiped out all the time.

Three months later I was pregnant again! I think I might have seriously considered killing myself if I hadn't felt so responsible for the two boys. When I went to the obstetrician he just looked so sorry for me and said, "If things were different I could just take you into the hospital and perform a D&C and no one would be the wiser, but lately they've been checking all D&C's to make sure they're not abortions." So I just put on my best grin-and-bear-it face. I think somehow I just thought it must be my fate, like Sisyphus, to be forever pushing uphill.

I had a very beautiful daughter, but three children in two and a half years is not something anyone should have to endure, including the children. When people ask me what it was like to have them all so close together I used to joke about it and say, "I don't remember." The fact is, I don't remember a lot of it. I was in a daze. At one point I remember figuring out that I hadn't slept through the night in three years. That does terrible things to your disposition. The children suffered a lot because I was stretched so thin. How can you be patient when you're exhausted and depressed and unhappily married? I'd feel so guilty . . . Every night when I put them all to bed I'd look at them and promise myself I would try to be more patient with them. I loved them all so much, but I just couldn't seem to hold it together. Of course now I see why. The constant emotional drain was so overwhelming, and there was no support or comfort for me. My husband would walk through the door at night and demand dinner, and then plop in front of the TV and stay there in a·trance for hours. I was very lonely. I had some close women friends, but they all seemed to be happier than I was, so as usual I figured it must be me. After all, I had always been so rebellious and dissatisfied. . . .

So it went for years. I was so determined not to admit defeat that I couldn't leave. Besides, where could I go? I had no way of making a living, and I knew Bruce would not agree without a terrible battle. In private he said really awful, abusive, degrading things to me about being stupid, demanding, selfish, a terrible mother, anything he could think of that would hurt. He was absolutely ruthless that way. When I fought back he resorted to physical violence. Not often; once or twice a year he would throw me across the room just to remind me of his control over me. I was really afraid of him.

One Christmas after we had been married for about six years we had a big fight and he attacked me and injured my back, and I ended up being taken to the hospital in an ambulance. I was in terrible pain for a month, and I never stopped hating him after that for intimidating me with his physical strength.

Then, once in a while he would act as if he couldn't live without me, buy me something wonderful, write me a love letter, or beg my forgiveness for the way he had acted. At these times, he would tell all our friends how much he adored me and they would tell me how lucky I was. One more time, I'd try to believe the romance and pray for better times.

After the seven-year mark I promised myself I would only stay long enough to get the kids through high school, and I started thinking about what the consequences would be if I tried to leave. I was terrified about having to make a living, because I knew there was no way I could support three kids. There was no network. There was no way of talking about this with other women.

Some time during the late sixties a good friend of ours, a man, gave me a copy of Betty Friedan's book, *The Feminine Mystique*. It hit me like . . . a lightning bolt . . . Revelation! It wasn't me! It wasn't that I was selfish and ungrateful. Other women felt the same, discontented and restless and trapped. I remember I had trouble finding anyone to talk with about the book. Everyone seemed a little afraid to get too close to anything that smacked of "women's lib," even though a lot of my friends actually had far more equal relationships with their husbands than I did. But the ideas sort of lodged there, and they worked on me over the next few years.

Of course, the whole sexual revolution was taking hold by then: open marriage, *Bob and Carol and Ted and Alice*, Make Love Not War, and I wanted to be part of it. I got a part-time job so I could pay for a babysitter myself, and get out of the house. I immediately met a number of very attractive, very successful men who apparently thought I was terrific. I had an affair and discovered just how fabulous it could be with a man who knew how to be sensitive and considerate about sex. A sensitive man! That was a whole new idea for me.

From then on, until the end of my marriage, I had a lover I could turn to every once in a while. It took the pressure off Bruce to perform sexually, which was completely beyond him, and it allowed me to stay married, because I didn't feel so angry and frustrated all the time. I had this secret life. The trouble was, I felt guilty all the time and sort of depraved about even being interested in sex, and then there was always the fear of getting caught. After a few years though, I sort of began to suspect that Bruce was relieved enough about being off the hook that he would never call me on it. He seemed incapable of jealousy, to the point of blindness. As long as the guy didn't move in with us. I would always choose a man I knew was not free—no possibility of commitment. I couldn't have done that: leave one man for another. So, I kept getting myself deeper into this sort of spiral [circling with her hand]: guilt, anger, frustration, depression. But at the same time, I saw it.

Finally, in 1972, when the kids were all settled in school, I went back to finish my B.A. degree. My husband alternated between being proud of me and freaked out. He always insisted that I was book-smart, but I had no common sense. You know, the perfect dumb blonde sort of image. Smart airhead. What more could any successful, ambitious man want?

I went to school full time, finally, and I loved it. I took a Psychology of Women course, and I met an interesting young woman who said she was in therapy, and she said I should try it, I would really enjoy it. I got up my courage and managed to convince my husband it was worth paying for. I think he liked the idea that now he could say I was the one who was crazy.

The woman I went to was a quiet feminist. I cried for about the first three sessions, mostly from relief, I think. Then I joined a group, and they were great, cheering me on. I told Bruce I wanted a divorce very soon after I started therapy. He was absolutely shocked. He thought our marriage was fine and he was furious. I wanted him to go for help with me. I begged him, but he quit after two or three sessions. Finally I told him it was either do something about getting help or I would have to leave. He said, "I'll do anything. Just don't ask me to change." Is that a classic? I knew that was the end. Even at the time it sounded hilarious. Unfortunately, it didn't end there. He was really vindictive, and in a rage about being rejected.

He kept suing me: for custody, for less child support, to get the house away from me. The custody battles went on and on. The kids were torn between us, and I was really concerned about the damage that was being done to them. He told them that if they didn't come to live with him he wouldn't see them anymore, because going back and forth wasn't "good for them." Finally, they gave in to the pressure and said they wanted to live with him. I knew if the kids were forced to testify against me in court it would put a wedge between us that I might never be able to repair. How could they ever admit they were wrong? How could I ever forgive them?

I've never recovered from losing my children. It seemed like such a bitter punishment for wanting to grow. I wanted to take them with me. I just didn't want to stay with their father. I couldn't change the fact that I had married a man I couldn't love or respect.

My daughter is trying to reestablish a relationship with me, but it's hard for her. She has all those years of conflict and torn-between feelings to overcome. I know she loves me and wants to have a mother, but the old stuff really gets in the way for her sometimes. It does for the boys, too.

People have said to me, "How can you be in favor of abortion? If you'd had one, you wouldn't have these beautiful children." But I would have had them. I just would have had them later. And I would have found a nicer man to be their father. I would have been more prepared and all our lives would have been so much easier.

Linda

At sixty-seven, she is a client relations executive for a prestigious art and antiques auction house in San Francisco.

Her home is in the Bay Area hills. In the entryway of the house there is an old-fashioned Coke chest, bright red. Beside it are wooden cases, stacked five feet high, filled with Coke in green glass bottles, the Classic ones. Billie Holiday is singing the blues in the background. As we begin to talk, my attention is diverted by the lyrics:

> Mama may have
> And Papa may have
> But God bless the child
> Who has his own . . .

Before I tell you about the circumstances of having an illegitimate child, I'll tell you about what led up to it.

The first abortion I had was in 1945 or '46. Something like that, and I was in New York City. I had just gotten out of the Navy and I was married, but we were not living together. He was in St. Louis, I was in New York, and we saw very little of each other. I wasn't ready to be married, first of all, even though I was old enough. I was twenty-seven or so.

I found myself pregnant and I was unsure who the father was, so I was too afraid to have the child. My husband knew I was pregnant, but he thought the child was his. I never told him anything different. I told him I was going to get an abortion. He pleaded with me not to, but I went ahead anyway . . . I felt I had to. A friend of mine who sort of knew the underworld made the arrangements for me. It was on Staten Island. We went there on the ferry together and whoever the contact was had told us to be at a certain restaurant. I don't even remember the name anymore and I doubt that I could even find the place. They left my friend there. They picked me up in a car and took me to a house and brought me to a room and a table and I don't know what they used. Afterward they told me to rest for a couple of minutes, so I did, and then they took me back to the restaurant and I met my friend and went back home. The next day I got very sick and ran a high fever and I went to the hospital. They asked there about what I had done, and I said I hadn't done anything, because we had been told that if anything happened we were not to say anything. They wouldn't be responsible . . . they'd say they never heard of us. So I went to the hospital and they gave me a D&C. I was there two or three days and swore I'd never have another abortion. I remember how frightened I was, thinking that this could kill me and feeling that I had to do it anyway and not knowing who the people were, and not being able to retrace my steps even if I had wanted to. No matter what had happened, I don't think I would have reported them because I felt that they were necessary . . . these abortion people.

After that, several years later, I was at home, in North Carolina, living on the farm with my mother. I got pregnant and I wasn't able to find an abortionist. I just went everywhere, and couldn't find anyone. There was . . . at that time . . . there was a family who lived on the farm. I went over to talk to the woman and I told her I was pregnant, asking her please not to tell my mother, and she said, "Let me think about it." Her sister was visiting her from Detroit, and the sister said that she thought she could do it. So I went over there and I guess she used a hatpin, I don't know what she used, something. Again, I got very sick and really scared, because I didn't want my mother to find out. My mother called the doctor because my fever was very high. The doctor came in . . . at that time doctors visited the home, and said he wanted to examine me alone. I told him what I had done, and I made him promise that he wouldn't tell my mother. He immediately went outside and told my mother and said, "We've got to get this girl into the hospital right away."

Well, we lived out in the country about eighteen miles from the nearest hospital, so he called an ambulance, and my mother came to the hospital and said, "Why on earth would you do such a thing?" And I said, "I just couldn't have the baby." I wasn't married and so . . . I have blocked a lot of this out of my mind, I really have, I don't think I've thought about much of it for a long, long time.

My mother wasn't too bad, really. She was a lot more understanding than I thought she would have been. She had had baby after baby. I don't think they ever used birth control. Maybe she didn't even know about birth control, I don't know. Or maybe my father was too demanding. She had seven children. So I think she was just shocked that I could do something like this, but even so, she didn't really carry on. She didn't try to make me feel worse than I did already. She was concerned . . . she wanted to know who did it . . . the abortion. And I refused to say, because I knew that it would just be horrible on those people, so there was no way I could say who it was . . . I wouldn't say. And after that, I was relatively free of abortion.

My mother wanted me to stay on the farm, but I went to live in San Francisco. I got married again and had a son, but when he was a baby my husband left me. Later, I got pregnant again. But at that time, I felt that I could not have an abortion, I just coudn't go through it again. The doctors in the hospital had told me how dangerous it was, that I could have died from those two abortions, and I was afraid. I just couldn't face abortion again. All my friends told me I was nuts, that I should have an abortion, or if I couldn't do that, then I should put the child up for adoption. Many of them pointed out all the troubles I would have, and many of them I've had, but I knew that I couldn't give it up, there was no way that I could put it up for adoption, that I was going to have to have an abortion or have a baby. So I had a daughter out of wedlock, but I wanted people to think she was legitimate. I couldn't face the trauma of people knowing I didn't have a husband. There was no way I could tell anyone at work about it. I knew I'd lose my job, so I didn't tell anyone except my best friend there. I had already arranged this with a friend of mine in Arizona. I was going to go out there for a week and then come back to San Francisco and have the baby. So I went out, stayed a week, and while I was there my ex-husband called work. I had told my boss that this friend of mine didn't have a phone, which was a lie. The woman I was staying with was the wife of the man who had "given me away" when I got married, so my ex-husband knew if I was in Arizona, that's where I was. He called and he said, "As long as you don't feel well, why don't you let me keep Bobby, and let him go to school in Kansas City." I thought that would be an ideal solution because I didn't want Bobby to know either. He was six. I felt that somehow I'd have things ironed out after a while, so I let Bobby go, and came back to San Francisco and holed up in my apartment. I just didn't go out, except for my visits to the doctor, and my boss kept sending telegrams saying that I was needed back at work, when would I be back at work? I would just call once in a while and say that I'd gotten his message, and that it would be another week or so, or two weeks, or something. Finally, I went to the doctor and I said, "Look, I just can't postpone it anymore. I've got to get back to work." So he induced labor, and I had the baby. I had the baby in a hospital out of town. After about four days I went back to work and left this baby out there with a lady who took care of infants. And I would go out at the end of the day, go out every weekend, and in the meantime, I had gotten Bobby back. I started telling him that we were going to adopt a little sister. Bobby told me later that he knew the score anyway, that he just went along with me.

In about six months I was able to get a house that I was negotiating for. I picked up the baby and I moved in with the two children and I've been there ever since. Everyone just assumed I was divorced and I had two children. That's what I had hoped they'd assume. I never talked about it, but it's just been that way. All my neighbors have never known me without two children. They've watched them grow up. I don't know what they think. I've never been one that runs in and out of houses anyway. When Bobby was eight or nine, he went to visit his father during the summer. Bobby told him he had a little sister, and my ex-husband took my son away from me. You know, he called me up and just accused me of having had a child in Puerto Rico when I went down there. He assumed that this child was mine.

He accused me of being an unfit mother and tried to take my son away from me. He literally kidnapped him. I couldn't find them. I had to hire a detective to go out there and get him. All of this led to the fact that Bobby doesn't see his father anymore. His father completely disowned him after that. He decided that if I could have a baby out of wedlock, that maybe Bobby wasn't his either. The boy hasn't seen his father since then.

Christina gets very angry at me. She has a terrible temper, and when she's mad she says, "Why did you ever have me? Why didn't you have an abortion?" I tell her that I did what I thought was right at the time. My daughter has been in and out of . . . I mean, she's had a couple of nervous breakdowns. . . .

Both of my children have had pretty rough lives. I had to hide my daughter. I had to pretend at work. I lived a lie for years. I was afraid to even let her answer the phone, because people at work didn't know I had two children. When she got to be about six years old my ex-husband called me and said that he was going to write a letter to where I worked and tell them what kind of character they had working for them, and make me lose my job. I wrote them a letter the next day and I talked to the president. I said, "I want you to know that I have another child, and my ex-husband is going to write a very nasty letter about me." And I expected to be fired, but he said, "Linda, since I'm somewhat of an old rake myself, if I get a letter like that it will just go right in the wastebasket. But," he said, "the one that you'll have to deal with is the vice-president, because he's the one who will never forgive you and never understand, so we'll have to find some way of telling him." I don't know who told him, but he never acknowledged my daughter . . . he's dead now, but he pretended she didn't exist.

I'm sure I was talked about. But I started talking about my daughter then. I started bringing her in. What they said behind my back I don't know, but little by little she was accepted. I've been there ever since, and now I doubt that many people even remember, because most of them are no longer there, and so there's nothing else to explain. But in those days, that was something you did not do. Just absolutely did not do it. And today, it's nothing. Women have babies without husbands all the time and no one bats an eyelash, but then it was considered immoral.

Colleen

"When I was eight I was sent away to live in a boarding-house with eight other children. I was very insecure, I felt unloved and unwanted, but I must have been popular in school in spite of that, because I was voted president of the whole eighth grade. But because I was a girl, the administration wouldn't accept it. They made a boy the president and I was vice-president. A little thing like that was a very big thing in the formation of my life: the feeling that being a girl, I was unworthy and unable to take things into my own hands. I was not trained to use my own mind to save myself or to change things. I'm fifty-seven years old, and I've finally learned that I can do these things for myself."

Jack Reilly . . . he used to beat the dog with a shovel, kick him down the stairs. When his car pulled in the driveway, the dog hid behind the biggest chair he could find, and the kids ran to their rooms. And I ended up spending fifteen years with this man. . . .

When I was in my twenties I had a super job as the right-hand gal and secretary to a very, very famous man of the time, I won't mention his name. At twenty-five, I was cruising around with a lot of stars and celebrities, and I was catered to a lot. I lived on Park Avenue in the Hotel Delmonico, and I had gotten into a world where I didn't know whether people were lavishing all these things on me because of the position I was in, or because they really liked me. I didn't know if they were being nice to me so they could get a plug in his column, or an act on his show. Jack had been a friend in high school. When I met him again and went out with him and he said he loved me, I thought, "Now this guy really loves me, he has nothing to gain." When I found out I was pregnant, the shame was so unbearable I never told anyone except the mother of a girl I had gone to secretarial school with. She was like an aunt to me, and she was the house nurse at the Hotel Roosevelt. She used to tell me rumors about how Jackie Gleason and Arthur Godfrey used to get all these girls pregnant and somehow this doctor she worked with knew where to send these girls to get them "fixed." It was sort of a New York show biz problem, and they thought nothing of it. So I called my girlfriend's mother and I told her. She said to bring a specimen to the hotel and she would have it analyzed for me. She was the one who told me I was pregnant, and I remember I was sitting in my boss's apartment at the Delmonico, talking on the phone to the Roosevelt, and thinking, "Oh, my God, I hope the switchboard operator isn't listening." I was so embarrassed, so ashamed. A twenty-six-year-old girl—I was so ashamed. But she wasn't any help. Apparently this doctor needed thousands and thousands of dollars to do abortions, and it was illegal, of course. I remember saying, "Isn't there something you can do?" But she couldn't.

If abortion had been legal that first time around, I never would have married Jack. Never. I knew abortion wasn't a "nice" thing to do, but I would have done it. I didn't love him. I didn't even look up to him in any way, and he certainly wasn't a "catch." My life would have been very different. I would have been spared the fifteen years of terror in marriage.

Jack had a history of unemployment for stretches of two or three years. We would live in homes where we would end up not being able to pay the rent after three months, but he was a wheeler-dealer, and he would call the landlords up and say, "Let us stay here. We'll clear the land," or "We'll do over the kitchen." So we'd end up staying, but with no money for food.

We couldn't have jelly on our toast in the morning because I needed the jelly to make peanut butter sandwiches for the kids' lunches.

Every day was either a physical or emotional torment. Jack started drinking a lot; he started dating other women openly; if his breakfast eggs weren't right, if the yolk broke I'd get slapped; he went after my son all the time. I tried to leave him two or three times, but with two children where could I go? I was completely alone, and I was terrified of what he was going to do. There was no such thing as a shelter for women in those days. Shelter. What a wonderful word. There was nowhere I could go that someone would stick up for me and protect me if he came to the door.

In those years, people didn't talk about things. There was nothing in the media or in any books about all the things that have happened to me: conceiving a child out of wedlock, having a son with schizophrenia, having an abusive husband, getting a divorce. These were things that were swept under the rug, and now everyone writes books about the things I used to try and hide.

I had been living in an isolated, insane world. I didn't even know if there was a war on. I had my own war. Finally, I decided that I would have to get a job, so I went back to business school and they sent me on interviews and I got a job at IBM corporate headquarters in New York. I was back with normal people doing normal things, and I was making six hundred dollars a month. That was a lot of money then.

I really wanted to leave Jack very badly then, but I was terribly afraid of him. I never knew what he might do. I found a lawyer and I had already met with him several times to talk about getting a divorce when I found out I was pregnant again. I called the lawyer and told him and he said, "Well, you only have two choices. You either get an abortion or you don't." He said, "Of course you can't get an abortion in the United States"—it was illegal—"but you can go to Sweden, or Puerto Rico." I opted for Puerto Rico. There was a clinic in San Juan.

The doctor there had been trained in the United States, and it was a completely legitimate operation. I didn't know how I was going to pay for the whole thing: the plane fare, the hotel, the abortion. The attorney contacted my father and he said he would pay all the bills. I was too embarrassed and upset to even tell him myself.

For legal reasons, the attorney didn't want it to appear that I was abandoning my family, just taking off like that. He advised me to write a letter to the babysitter, including her advance pay for two or three weeks. I was to tell her I was going away, and she should come to watch the two children as usual. I had it all ready to mail so that it would arrive at the house on the day I was leaving.

The attorney arranged for the airplane tickets, and a reservation in a San Juan hotel. He advised me to take my clothes out of the house a little bit at a time, and keep a suitcase at the office or in a woman friend's car or something, so that the day I left the house I would be leaving without anything. I told my boss that I had had a phone call and there was a family emergency of some kind out in the Midwest, and I would be back in ten days, no more than two weeks. In San Juan, the clinic was closed on Saturday and Sunday, so I remember I found a very lovely little Catholic church that looked like a monastery with adobe walls, very Spanish, and I went there on Sunday.

Monday morning I went to the clinic. You didn't need appointments, you'd just go and wait in the waiting room. The doctor took some history. I'd had two Caesarian deliveries, and I could not tell for certain how many months pregnant I was because I was always under so much stress that I wasn't very regular. I really wanted him to know that this was something I didn't take lightly. This was survival for myself and the children. I would lose my job! And then I'd have three children to take care of. What was I to do? I finally had the means to leave Jack and take care of my children. This was really for all of us. But the clincher was that the doctor told me I couldn't get an abortion without my husband's permission; he would have to sign for it! I told him that the reason I came all the way down here was to get *away* from the man! I couldn't hop a plane and go back and have him sign this! I cried and I wept and I begged him to do it anyway. My father's signature, or some other responsible person? And he said no. He never examined me. I never got further than his office, and he begged me not to go to any other abortion place in Puerto Rico. "There are people who would give you the abortion, especially since you're paying cash, and they just won't care," he said. "If you love your own two children, don't go anyplace else. You have had two Caesarians, which means you have a ropelike scar on the inside of the uterus, and any kind of scraping of the uterus would disrupt that scar tissue. You could bleed internally, and you'd be asking for death."

It just occurred to me that maybe he really didn't want to do it because it was dangerous, and just threw in this part about the signature. I mean, I can see I have a scar on the outside of my stomach, so I must have one on the inside too.

When I realized that I couldn't get him to change his mind, I left, and I remember going back to the Catholic church where I'd been the day before. It was a hot day, muggy, and the church was cool and deserted. I just knelt down and wept and wept and wept.

When I got back, I went to my father's home, and there I found out what my husband had been doing while I was gone. He had had me tailed! As soon as I didn't come home from work he called IBM and my boss said I'd gone to visit the relatives. My husband knew that wasn't true, so he'd called a detective and had all the airports checked, and I was tailed everywhere I went in Puerto Rico! He went crazy with anger. He found a telephone book with all my friends' names in it that I'd had for years, and he called everyone and said, "Do you know what kind of a girl Colleen is really?" And told them all where I was and what I was up to. Then he marched into IBM and accused my boss of being the father of the child, and brought in a big brown paper grocery bag full of pens and pencils and steno pads and notepads—anything that could relate to being a secretary—and he said I had stolen all these things from IBM, and turned this grocery bag upside down on my boss's desk.

I was afraid to go back to the house. But the two children were there with him, and I was afraid of running the risk of losing them if I didn't go back. He had told the children that I had left them because I didn't love them and that I would never be back. Two little kids, three and six, and he was poisoning them against me even then. They didn't know what the word abortion meant, but he told them that I was going to kill their little brother or sister, that's what I was up to. I was afraid to go back; I was so afraid. I get the same feeling in my chest now that I'm talking about it . . . I was so afraid.

IBM wrote to me—of course, they heard the whole story from Jack—and said that they were sorry I'd been through such difficulties, but under the circumstances they felt it would be better if I didn't come back. They didn't want me in that job with him around. They paid me severance pay, but I couldn't go back.

It seemed like such an eternal struggle. I was very naïve. The communication between women during the fifties and sixties was just nonexistent. I thought I was the only one in the world that had this problem. No one ever wanted to admit that these bad things happened to them. So much was based on saving face. But the memories never go away. They hover around while you're making dinner or when you go by a store that sells little children's clothes. You think of your own children and the things that happened.

If I hadn't lost my job . . . But of course I didn't know how I would take care of this baby and go back to work. No one did that then, and the idea was so foreign to me, I just couldn't imagine how I could do it, so finally I went back and stayed with Jack and had this child. She was born blind and profoundly retarded, and I ended up staying with him for seven more years.

DESPERATE MEASURES

It is probable that induced abortion is a universal cultural phenomenon. Harry L. Shapiro, Ph.D., notes that out of 200 tribal dossiers in the Human Relations Area File at Yale, 125 contained positive records of the occurrence of abortion. In addition, a survey by Devereaux has listed more than 300 distinct tribal or cultural groups where induced abortion is known and practiced. In fact, he was able to identify only one group where it could be confidently said that induced abortion was unknown.

—Robert E. Hall, M.D., editor,
"An Anthropologist's View,"
Abortion in a Changing World

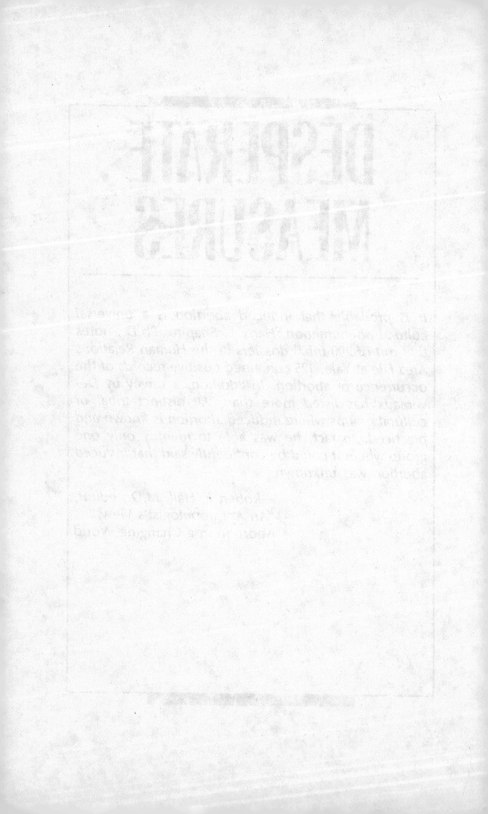

Joyce

I am in the presence of colorful oil paintings of flamboyant, larger-than-life people. Some are hanging, some are stacked against the walls. Joyce selects a few others for me to see. She is close to deadline, energetically preparing for a show, but takes time out to tell me her story. She speaks passionately about her fear that abortion is in danger of becoming illegal again, and wants very much to be a part of this book.

"I think it is so essential for women to have the choice of having a clinical abortion where you are safe, and where you are treated with dignity, you don't have to go through that terrible pain, and it doesn't cost all that money and you're not going to die if something goes wrong, and the guy's not going to run away and let you bleed to death."

I was brought up in a very conservative, middle-class Jewish household, where my whole reason to be was to be a mother. When I entered college, the advice that my mother gave me was, "Now you're going to college, and this is where you're going to meet your husband, and if you don't, you'll be in big trouble." And that was my entering college advice. So there was a lot going on about "Should I get married, should I not get married, should I do it?" . . . a lot of holes there. So, I don't know. Maybe I would have quickly married somebody else. It took me many years to get rid of that wife/mother myth. . . . But growing up in Brooklyn during the fifties was very one-directed for girls. There was only one thing that you were supposed to be interested in: boys.

We had no sex education at all, nothing. We learned by doing. I have a sister who's about five years older than I am, who didn't know anything either. I remember when I was a little kid, she had a girl friend who supposedly knew things, and one night my parents went out, and my sister was baby-sitting—I think she must have been about fourteen—and they ran after me telling me how you have a baby, and I ran under my mother's bed [laugh]. That was about the limit of my sex education. When I was ten or so, I asked my mother how you have babies, and she told me: "The stork brings them—how do you think?" When I was eleven, I got my period, and I showed my mother. I said, "Ma, look." I wasn't sure, I mean, I thought I knew, but I wasn't sure. She said, "Well, I suppose you know what that is." So I said, "Yes, I suppose I do." But it was so embarrassing that I couldn't say to her, "No, I don't understand what it is," because it was easier for me emotionally than what I would have to go through with my mother to say, no I don't know. I had never talked with my family about sex. Sex was always a bad thing unless you were married.

When I was eighteen, and my boyfriend at the time was also eighteen, I became pregnant. I was astonished . . . I had never expected that I would become pregnant. I mean, we were careful and all that, but I never really made the connection emotionally. I understood intellectually that there was a connection between sex and pregnancy, and I understood the physical processes, but the real emotional understanding that I could conceive a child just wasn't there. Anyway, I got pregnant and we were both hysterical, and I wanted to get married as the way out, but David didn't. He felt it would ruin his life and our life and everybody's life . . . which was probably true, because later we got married and I'm divorced now [laughs]. So we set a date, and in the meantime I had gone to the library. I had not told anyone in my family, especially my mother. We had a very poor relationship all our lives—all my life—so she would be the last one that I would ever think of to go to for help. I had gone to the library and I took out a book about abortion and sex and all kinds of stuff, and—I realized this later—I left it on the kitchen table, which is very funny, now I laugh, but at the time obviously it was a way to say "help." So, finally we were getting close to getting married and David was just beside himself, and I was seeing that there just was no way that I was going to go through with this, so at the last minute I agreed to have an abortion. I had no idea about how to go about getting an abortionist or anything. I had known a girl who had had several abortions, but she had been taken by her mother to some clinic in Philadelphia, and her mother had some kind of distant connection with the Mafia, and so they had everything arranged. That was the only abortion I had known about. When I saw that it was the only way, I finally agreed, but I was so terrified because I just didn't know what to expect.

So David, through his older sister, through someone or other, got the name of a doctor in Brooklyn. We lived in Brooklyn, in Borough Park. We made an appointment with the doctor through all kinds of surreptitious means, and it was finally agreed that I would go at a certain time—around one o'clock in the afternoon. I was to have the abortion in the doctor's office, and it was to cost $750. This was in 1958, so you can imagine how expensive $750 was. I had some money in my savings, and David had been working for a number of years and had a little money. We pooled our money and made the appointment, and we were to meet a man on the corner where I lived. He would pick David and me up in a car, which we were given a description of. We were to give this man $100 and he would take us to the doctor's office. Well, about a day or so before I went, I told my mother. It's very interesting, because she was always very hysterical, and we had a bad relationship, and everything I did was bad and horrible and no good, but strangely enough, in this case she was very supportive and sympathetic, which really shocked me to death. You can't imagine, because you don't know this relationship. She walked with us out to the front door, which was a lot for her. We got into the car and the guy in the car gave me a couple of pills to take, to "calm me down," he said.

I had no idea what they were, but whatever they were, I would have taken them. I was in no psychological position to question anything, and David was so terrified and so relieved at the same time, that he was just, you know, "Take it."

So, we get to the doctor, and it's a very nice doctor's office in Borough Park, in Brooklyn. He's got a nice practice that's clean and normal. He takes me into the office. David waits outside, I just take off my underpants and lie on the table in the stirrups, and he gives me the abortion without any anesthesia whatsoever. He scraped, I guess he did a curettage. It was so painful that you can't imagine. He said it only will last fifteen minutes, the whole operation. So, he did the operation . . . it was the most unbelievable, painful thing, and I just remember in the middle of it, screaming for my mother . . . because it was just terrible. At the end of the operation, he said to me, "Do you want to see it?" I said, "No, of course not!" So he said, "Okay, go and lie down for a couple of minutes," and he gave me a shot of penicillin, and I went into the inner office and lay down for a little while. But he did this operation in between his regular office hours, and in just a few minutes he wanted me to get out because he had a practice. David and the driver were in the outer office, and they took me home. My mother was waiting for me, and she just said, "Is everything all right?" and I said, "Yes," and I went upstairs and got into bed. I felt tremendous relief.

I remember my mother being very sympathetic, very, very sympathetic. I don't remember if she told my father, or whether he knew, or whether he did anything, but he just didn't seem to play any part in it.

The next morning, very early in the morning, David came over with this big, giant Teddy bear, and my mother said to him something to the effect of . . . "I'm surprised to see you here, I didn't expect to see you again" . . . something that was a com-

bination of horrible anger, and "Oh boy, I'm glad you're here."
I just remember him coming over that day, with such a look of
relief, and being so grateful to me. For the next six months
before we married, he was so nice to me—like I never remember him being before or after [laughing] because he was so
relieved. After the abortion, I was supposed to go back to the
doctor a few times for a checkup, and to take penicillin shots
and make sure there was no infection. I heal very rapidly, and
there was no problem, except that I remember going back after
the first or second week and he gave me an examination. My
breasts had been very swollen when I was pregnant, and this
bastard, who had asked me if I wanted to see the fetus, touched
my breasts and said, "Oh, well, they were better before."
Mnnnnhmmmm, sleaz-o. That's the general story.

Jacqueline

Jacqueline is a grandmother who looks younger than her nearly sixty years. Now divorced, she is a full-time college teacher.

Her living room, where we talk, is traditionally furnished, without sign of fad or fashion. There is a neatly stacked pile of The New York Times Magazine *on the table near the couch, which Jacqueline means to read when she "has the time."*

She speaks precisely in a modulated voice, but in contrast to her quiet manner, you sense an underlying toughness. A grandfather clock on her living room wall chimes the hour as Jacqueline begins her story.

I never knew anyone who had an abortion. None of my friends. No one had ever talked to me about it. If I knew about it, it was from hearing horror tales, or from novels. I had never heard of anything like what happened to me.

In the forties I went to a small women's college in Boston. My friend Irene was attending a special series for the students and heard a woman doctor, a gynecologist, speak on birth control. When I think back on it, it was really pretty remarkable that this was sponsored by a college for single women in the forties. The doctor talked about diaphragms. This all happens to be significant in terms of my story, because later I roomed with Irene.

I had been from a very conservative small town, and was a virgin and had strong convictions about maintaining my virginity until I was married. Irene fell in love with this young guy. It was such a small, tiny apartment. We had bunk beds, one dresser, a small closet, a teensy little kitchen and a living room. But it was on the back side of Beacon Hill in Boston, and we had a fireplace. This tiny little place had a style and a charm and a location. So here we lived, and she was going with Jim and they were obviously having a sexual relationship.

When we got the apartment I must have been twenty. About a year later I met a guy who was interning at one of the hospitals in the city. Dick and I had an immediate physical attraction. I think he picked up on it the second we met. Anyway, Dick and I, eventually, although I resisted for a while . . . started having an affair. I cried the first time, at the enormity of what I could experience. I was just overwhelmed. But I became aware that there were a lot of women in his life, that there had been, and maybe were others now. He acknowledged that he was not emotionally involved with me. We had been having this very passionate, very exciting sexual relationship, and it was so disappointing not to have love. I felt rejected. I wanted him to love me.

During this time I was taking an evening class at Harvard and a guy began sitting next to me. After some weeks, he put his hand on the back of my neck and began caressing me. And that was exciting too. It had never occurred to me that I could be excited by more than one male. Here I am, you know, how can this be? I wasn't paying too much attention to it until Dick said he didn't love me, and I felt really devastated. Here I'd given myself to this man and he didn't even love me.

And meanwhile this other guy from the class, whose name I don't even remember, began to be interested. He wanted me to go have a cup of coffee with him. We sat by the Charles River, I think it was fall. He was making overtures, and I was really very ambivalent about it. I guess what really appealed to me was his interest. We went up to the apartment. After my saying no for hours, he was ready to leave, and all of a sudden something in

me encouraged him to stay. We had sex, and suddenly I realized that all the time that Dick and I were having a relationship
he used condoms. This guy didn't have . . . I had no kind of
protection. So we had this one episode and I became pregnant.

My first reaction was, "Oh, God, what have I done?" Somehow in my emotional confusion I'd gotten involved with this
guy and I ended up pregnant.

My first reaction was really suicidal. I started contemplating
how to steal pills from the drug room at the hospital where I
worked. I was very depressed and I didn't know . . . There was
no way I could seriously consider turning to my family. I
couldn't think of anything else to do, commit suicide or have an
abortion. Those were the only two viable options as far as I was
concerned.

When I talked with Irene about it, she told me that she went
to a lecture on birth control by a woman doctor, and she
thought that this woman was aware of where abortions could be
performed. I guess there was some part of me that really wanted
to live, so I made an appointment with this doctor.

At that time they did the frog test. It was positive, and only
confirmed what I already knew. I went back to the doctor to ask
her if she could perform an abortion, or knew how I could get
one. She asked me if there wasn't some way that I could live
with this. She didn't know I was considering not living. Wasn't
there some way that I could go through with it? I said, "No
way." She said, "Your family?" and I said, "No way." I can
remember her saying, "You know sometimes families are more
supportive than you realize." I thought that one over. There
was no way.

When my mother and father were divorced, I was to go with
my mother, but my father had not sent her the support pay-
ments he was supposed to, so she sent me back to him. I grew
up with my father and my stepmother. I never remember my
father putting his arms around me, or holding me on his lap or
doing anything affectionate. My stepmother was very strict. I
always knew when I was doing something wrong; I never knew
when I was doing anything right with her. I grew up in this very

cold atmosphere, not supportive, not loving. There was no way I could go back to them and say, "I failed. I'm pregnant. Help me." In fact I had left home and gone into nursing only to get away. It was a way to escape and be independent.

So here I was, sitting in this office, saying the only thing for me was an abortion. The dramatic scene was when she finally conceded that maybe she could refer me to someone who would help me, but would not tell me this person's name. She took out the telephone book and took her letter opener and drew it down the page to this line, and said, "Here, read this." She would not say the name. It gave me this dramatic sense: my first sense of this backstreet criminal action I was about to take. This made it clear that there were some legal implications here and she was not going to involve herself in it.

The man was a urologist, and I think he had lost his license to practice. I went home and called him to make an appointment. He lived in an older, respectable but shabby neighborhood in which he had this large apartment. As far as I could figure out there wasn't anyone else there when I was. On the first visit he told me how much it would cost: one hundred dollars. He made it clear that if there were any complications he would disavow any connection with me.

One hundred dollars was a lot of money to me at the time, considering what my income was. I didn't have the money. And in the meantime I was still seeing Dick. So I told Dick that I was pregnant, and when I first told him, I didn't tell him the circumstances. He'd been very careful of course, but assumed he was responsible. He said, "What are we going to have, a shotgun marriage?" Immediately something happened to my ego. I guess he thought that's what I would want. I said no, I was going to have an abortion, so he volunteered to pay for it and I accepted.

On the first visit to this doctor, he inserted a catheter. He said that very often this initiated some contractions and made it easier to do an abortion. Sometimes that was all that was necessary, but it didn't work. So I had to go back for the abortion. Meanwhile Irene had talked this over with her boyfriend Jim, and Jim decided that I shouldn't go alone. He volunteered to go with me. Neither one of them ever tried to dissuade me from having an abortion. They were supportive. Dick felt let off the hook. He supported me by giving me the money to have it. He didn't volunteer to hang around, and I wasn't expecting him to, because I knew he wasn't responsible.

So, Jim went with me. I went in and he waited in the living room. I remember going into this room in his apartment and there was a table and stirrups. The thing that bothered me was the way he sterilized the instruments. He had this big basin of disinfectant. Wouldn't you think a physician who was a urologist who did surgery would have had a sterilizer? That bothered me. I wasn't too sure how he rinsed the instruments. I didn't have any anesthesia. To tell you the truth, I thought that maybe I was better off without it, since I had heard stories about people dying from the anesthesia being inappropriately administered during abortions. A part of me was addressing the procedure, and the rest of me was having it.

I remember the pain. It wasn't sharp, just a kind of deep cramping agony. And I guess a couple of times I kind of moaned a little, but mostly I was just quiet. Jim said afterward that this guy spoke to him, probably assuming that he was a participant in this pregnancy, and commented to Jim that he had never seen anyone as quiet as I was. He said they usually scream and this was a reason he had a top-floor apartment. He said there was usually a lot of screaming, and I wondered if he was disappointed.

We took a cab home, and I rested that evening. I recovered physically. I felt a little weak and wobbly for a few days, but I don't know if it was mostly psychological, or emotional, or whether it was really physical.

It was bothering me that Dick thought he was responsible for this, so I decided to level with him. I felt I owed it to him. I told him that he was not the father and he didn't believe me. I thought, "This is fine, he thinks I'm not capable of this."

I think I had the abortion in May, and after I went home that summer I realized what a depression I was in. It was the most awful, unpleasant experience I've ever had. I've never been as depressed since. It was this awful, flat feeling. I began to wonder if I was ever coming out of it. I did meet this sweet guy who was a relative of some friends of my parents, and just compulsively told him the whole story. We went out, had a couple of drinks and sat in his car, and I told him the whole damn thing. He was a good listener, but he did say to me, "Well, I usually don't give advice, but I have one piece of advice for you. I would suggest that you not tell strangers this story."

This was during World War II, and Dick was in the reserves stationed in New York. In the fall we got together for a cup of coffee, and he brought me a box of detergent. It seems like a funny present now, but at the time everything was rationed. He looked me over very carefully, and he said he had a real concern that I hadn't had the abortion, I'd only told him that I did. He found it difficult to conceive of me having an abortion, and that I was not the kind of person who would get involved with another guy because I was feeling rejected. He sort of mirrored all the things I wanted to believe about myself.

I think while I was depressed I was out of touch with the terrible hopelessness of the situation. The fear hadn't bothered me that much because I was sort of suicidal anyway, but there was a part of me that wanted to live. I had felt desperate, but I got over feeling desperate once I had a plan. I took care of myself, put that armor on and marched in there to do what I had to do [crying].

It wasn't unusual for me to feel that there was no one to turn to, since I'd felt that way most of my life. When I first found out I was pregnant it was spring, and I can remember leaning on the windowsill, spending a long day looking out the window, feeling desperate. I think that I cried off and on all that day, leaning against that windowsill. And that was the last time in all these years till now. I never knew another woman who had an abortion in those years. I felt that there was no one to turn to. Only in the past ten years did I know any other women who acknowledged they had had an abortion. My generation just did not talk about it.

Heather

"When you're dealing black market, you're stuck because you've got noplace else to go. You're afraid any minute the doctor's going to turn around and say, "Get out of here." And then what are you going to do? So you just let him go his merry rounds.

When abortion was illegal it was black market even if it was done in a hospital by a doctor, and you had letters from psychiatrists. I was not psychologically deranged, but they made me that way by the time I was done with this craziness."

My first abortion was approximately one month before abortion became legal. I had become pregnant on what was called the sequential birth control pill, which was given to me by a gynecologist because I was not ovulating. Instead of telling me that this was a high-risk thing, he gave me this birth control pill and said "Birth control," and I ended up pregnant.

When I went back to my gynecologist, who was the head of OB-GYN at a large metropolitan hospital, he yelled at me. He asked me what kind of birth control I was on, and I told him "sequential birth control pills," and he said, "Who was the idiot who gave you those?" and it was him! So he tried to cover that whole thing up and dragged my husband into it. We were young kids in our twenties, and newly married, and he said he wanted one thousand dollars cash—to "pay off the hospital board"—in a paper bag! And he bullied my husband by telling him that it would cost him a hell of a lot more to have this kid than to get rid of it. So I had to go take the money out of the bank and pay him cash, and see two psychiatrists that he gave me the names of, and pay them each one hundred dollars in cash to get them to type a letter saying that I was suicidal. It was as if my husband and this doctor were on the phone like cronies, consulting each other and that sort of thing. My husband's screaming, "We can't have this child . . . I don't have the money for this." And it was nuts, it was like a full moon or something, and I was the victim. And if I protested or said anything, the doctor would pooh-pooh me in front of my husband. It was like the "old boys" network.

It was weird. People were running in a hundred different directions. I should also mention that my husband was checking places for me to go. He had me ready to go to Haiti when the revolution broke out in Haiti, so I couldn't get an abortion there. He was going to fly me to England, because you could obtain an abortion there. So the process was something which seemed to take weeks of the most incredible and ridiculous effort involved in booking flights and travel agents and everything else, just to do what people now go to a local clinic for.

Finally, I went to the hospital and had the abortion. It was just a terrible mess. I was just there overnight—I got home and went into labor! I had terrible pain, and tried to call the doctor. We finally tracked him down at a restaurant. He told my husband that I was just being a big baby, but he agreed to give me a prescription. John went into Manhattan to get it at the restaurant, and while he was gone, a fetus came out of my body, which freaked me out. That was what just about drove me under. It was one thing to have an abortion and go through all this process, but to have to deal with the fetus! It was supposed to be a D&C but he did not remove the fetus. Later he insisted that I must have had twins and he had missed one. It really affected my mind, and the doctor just tried to cover it up, and he didn't recommend that I receive any help, and was constantly saying to my husband, "Oh, she's just being crazy."

During the follow-up examination, this doctor was on the phone with one of his colleagues and said, "Oh, hi, yeah, I'm here with all the girls with their legs up. You know me, I'm just a glorified plumber." I just got up off the table, and put my clothes on and walked out the door and went home. He called my house and wanted to know why I had left, and I said, "Look, I just decided I'm not a glorified sink," and I just would never go back.

This was such a shock all the way around. A doctor was supposed to be an authority figure; then you never questioned a doctor, a minister, a teacher, none of these people were ever questioned as they are today. He was a gynecologist, a ladies' doctor. I had assumed that he cared about me, but I felt betrayed. And I could never have disclosed this to my family, because they would have had total hysterics. It was like there was no place to go. You go through a whole period of something like mourning, because, it's like you're sabotaged by your husband, you're sabotaged by your own doctor, and you learn that those people that you think love you . . . you can't trust them. That's a shock to someone in their twenties. You don't have the experience of life to be able to handle all this at the same time, at least I did not.

For years, it was like there was no explaining it to myself. There were just emotional feelings that were incredibly negative. I have yet to be back to a gynecologist. I am forty-three years old, and it has taken me this long to get over that. I mean, it sounds crazy. I have never gone back.

You know there is a right to life for the woman . . . and for the husband who has his difficulties. It was not me who could not handle it psychologically, it was my husband, but no one ever assumes that it's the man who should say he's mentally deranged and he's going to kill himself. So, if you love him, to help your husband out you have to go and say, "Yes, I'm going to do myself in." One shrink was somewhere way the heck out in Bayside, Queens. I'll never forget it. It took half the day to get there by train. He was in an office that was like a closet with a window. He had a typewriter with an extension cord going out the window, plugged into another room. Here was this guy making these abortion letters, with his shingle on the wall. So while your husband is at the office having coffee with the boys, you're out there paying off shrinks who are typing away, saying, "What's your name again, honey?"

Mary

Mary is a talented hairstylist with a prosperous shop of her own in New York's Hudson Valley. With her curly, golden-red hair, see-through blue eyes, and stylish good looks, she exemplifies her craft.

When I had my illegal abortion, I was eight months out of high school. I had left home and I was going to community college. I went to a doctor to get birth control pills and I was waiting for my period. It didn't come, so then I had a pregnancy test and I found out that I was pregnant. I was eighteen. So after this doctor had given me the pregnancy test, I asked him about getting the abortion and stuff, and he told me about two different doctors that he knew of. He really would not be involved except to give me a phone number and this password. There was one doctor in New York City I called first but I didn't get through, so I called the one in Philadelphia and they gave me a date to show up and I guess they gave me an address. I went with my boyfriend and my sister. This place was in an abandoned neighborhood; all the buildings were empty. We went to the house; it was like a big old house. There were real tall ceilings in the entranceway. There was plastic furniture. The place was painted white, but it had been painted a long time ago. It was real dingy looking and it had green plastic chairs. Just sitting in that room there, nobody's talking to anybody. No communication at all. I was scared to death anyway, but then to show up in this kind of a place, it was completely out of my culture. First of all going to a supposed doctor and being in an abandoned building in a place that had . . . it was very dark and dank looking. My sister and my boyfriend were really freaked out. My sister later said, "I thought they were putting you to your death." They called my name and I went into this office. There was this guy in there and he was showing me some paperwork. I guess it was the doctor's licenses. He was telling me that the doctor was an abdominal surgeon, I guess to like ease your mind, that he was going to do a good job. The guy never told me his name. He told me he was there to represent the doctor. Anyway, he says to me, "You know you're not going to get an abortion today. Come back in a week and what you have to do is leave three hundred as a deposit and come back in a week," and I just looked at him and said, "Oh, my God." First of all, I said to myself, this is insane. I mean, I could leave my three hundred dollars and come back and there would be nobody here, ya know. And I said, "Wait a second, I thought this was going to be done today. I really tried to prepare myself. I got the money and I was told it was going to be done today. How do I know it's going to happen if I leave the three hundred dollars here?" He said, "Well, I'm sorry, you're just going to have to take my word for it. That's the way it's going to be." So I said, "Wait a second, I'll be right back," and I walked out and I went to get my boyfriend and my sister. He wouldn't let them come in and discuss anything which, at the time, I didn't quite understand. Now looking back on it, I think it's because of legal reasons, because if anything did happen, it was my word against his. So we left and went outside the room and discussed it between ourselves and we decided we'd leave the money 'cause I felt at that point that I had no other option. If I was going to get the abortion—the other doctor had told me this doctor was good, and other people had gone there—I figured that I may as well take my chances. So that's what we did, and we came back a week later. They called my name and they took me upstairs. I remember these long stairs and then there were a lot of rooms.

They put me in one of these rooms and they sat me down on a table. They gave me a shot which put me out real quick. And the nurse—I'll never forget the nurse. She had a lot of makeup on and this very dyed black hair; she didn't have a nurse's uniform on.

I really don't have any idea how long it must have been. At the end of my table they had a TV blasting. This TV was so loud! When I woke up, I was really conked out from the drugs, but the TV being so loud was really driving me nuts, and I just wanted to get over there and turn that TV off, and it seemed like it took me forever to get out of the bed because I was, you know, drugged. So I finally managed to get myself out of the bed and I turned the TV off, and then I had to go to the bathroom. This room had a couple of doors in it. I went over to one door, and I opened the door and there was another abortion going on and the woman was screaming. The doctor turned around to me and said, "What the hell are you doing in here? Get out of here!" I said, "No problem." Then the nurse came in and said to me, "What are you doing out of bed?" I said, "I have to get out of here." She said, "You have to stay in bed because you have to let the drug wear off." I was in really bad shape. It was like being in the middle of a Fellini movie. Is this really happening to me? You know that kind of feeling of being outside yourself. I got to the top of the stairs and my sister and my boyfriend were sitting in the living room, and they took one look at me and I could see by their eyes that they thought I was going to die. They came up the stairs and grabbed my arms and they carried me out to the car and put me in the backseat. I was sprawled out in the backseat and I felt really sick. When I left there nobody really said anything to me; no instructions about what to do or what to expect. They told me what they were going to do beforehand, that time when I went in and left the money. They told me that you were scraped and this and that. There was an option; you could get the abortion without being put out; if you weren't put out it was cheaper. I did not want to be awake, and after hearing that woman scream in the next room, I was glad I made that decision. Later, I called the doctor who had given me this doctor's name. I asked him if he would give me a checkup and he said no. I asked him why not and he told me that he couldn't get involved in this. I begged him and finally he agreed and I went to get the checkup. He said, "You're fine." I sort of felt like, hey, you know, I shouldn't have had to beg you to give me an examination. I mean, after all, I am your patient. You'd think that he'd be concerned. He said that as long as I was feeling all right, I must be fine. Other people went there and they're fine. I said to him, "This place was horrible that you sent me to. Why didn't you tell me it was going to be so horrible?" And he said to me, "If I told you how horrible it was going to be, would you have gone?" And I said probably not. "So that's why I didn't tell you."

Ethel

Ethel was referred to us by her daughter, a rabbi's wife. She is a reserved and soft-spoken woman in her eighties. A second-generation Jewish immigrant, she grew up on the Lower East Side of New York City. The story she tells took place there, in a neighborhood where families were close, and "all you had to do was ask."

It was more than I bargained for. I was nineteen, and I already had a child of my own. It wasn't the right time. I was very young. I just didn't want another child at that time. It wasn't right. This was in the early twenties. My husband was a salesman on the Lower East Side.

They were bad times. That was the main reason. People didn't have enough money to take care of the families they had. Oh, they were married women. I never knew any single women who had abortions. Maybe there were, but I didn't know them.

Everybody cared about each other. That's true. I don't find it that way anymore. It's very different now. You had to be friends, family never knew about this thing. You never told family.

One of my friends told me about it, I don't recall who it was, one of my neighbors. There was a lot of information. If you were in trouble, you asked and you got the answer, privately. You felt you were going to a doctor who knew what he was about to do. A couple of people I knew had done it, so you felt almost safe.

It wasn't cheap to have it done. I thought you might be interested in that. It was fifty dollars. Oh, there were some who had it done cheaper than that. My price was fifty dollars. At the time it was a lot of money. It was a week's pay for most people. But everybody could somehow get their hands on a fifty-dollar bill. If it cost more than that I guess people wouldn't do it. There were some women who were performing abortions, but they weren't doctors. They said they were nurses, that's what they said, but you couldn't prove it. They were doing it for maybe twenty or twenty-five dollars. I heard talk about them. My friends didn't go to those people. And I wouldn't have considered it. Maybe because I was afraid. Maybe because my husband wouldn't hear of it.

We had agreed, we both agreed. I wanted it done, so he went along with me. We were both very young. He was just three years older. We had met in school. There were many doctors who did it in those days, although they didn't talk about it. They were not allowed to do it. The doctors weren't making too much money in those days. This was a great source of income. You could see a doctor for a dollar. When he got a fifty-dollar bill it was a lot of money. There were a lot of Jewish doctors who would treat women—the immigrants.

In those days, all you had to do was ask. Maybe some women didn't have the money to pay the doctor. That's it. They had no money so they couldn't have it done. So they had to go to some quack for five or ten dollars. It only took fifteen or twenty minutes. Even a doctor would tell you where to go. If you were his patient and he didn't do it, he knew of doctors who did. And he would tell his patient, "I don't do it," he'd tell you, "Here's a doctor." And he'd give you an address and you would go. This was his patient, he wanted her to have it done. But he wasn't doing it, so he wasn't going to get into any trouble.

Later, I did have two more children. But at the time it wasn't right.

I never thought about it after that. In the beginning, maybe, yes, for a while. But I really never think about it. Especially now—what's to think about?

Nancy

There can be a thin line between what is real and what you have to pretend is real.

In order to meet the legal requirements for a therapeutic abortion, Nancy had to claim that her mental stability was threatened by the enormous stress of her mother's impending death and her family's history of psychosis. This charade threatened to validate her worst fears: that she too might be crazy.

What I had to feel was crazy. The circumstances of my abortion were extremely emotionally fraught. I found out I was pregnant the same day I found out my mother had three weeks to live. She was dying of cancer. Both my parents had found out they had cancer on the same day three years before. My stepfather died soon after that, and my mother lived for three more years. It was clearly a hard time for me.

I got involved with a man. It was the beginning of a relationship and I was fond of him—but I had this gut feeling I didn't want to marry him, didn't want to spend the rest of my life with him. I didn't want to have children with him. I had thought I was pregnant before New Year's. I remember having gone to a New Year's Eve party and getting violently ill afterward. The next day feeling horrible—just horrible, and I hadn't had anything to drink. I just felt very sick and I thought, "I bet I *am* pregnant." The day after New Year's I got two phone calls:

the doctor saying, "Yes indeed, you are pregnant," and the other one was my grandmother saying, "We've been trying to get in touch with you for a couple of days, your mother's cancer has spread to her liver and she has three weeks to live." And I remember just being numb—just realizing I could not in any way have a baby.

Once or twice prior to the pregnancy I had seen a therapist—the same therapist my mother was seeing. I called her and said, "I'm pregnant. What am I going to do? I want an abortion, can you help me?" and she said, "No. I've heard of a clinic, someplace in Pennsylvania, but I don't know the name." The first call was basically, "You're on your own." And I think that I made a couple of calls back to her. I don't know if she realized at that time that my mother was dying. When she found out she said, "Well, there is something I can do. I will write a letter and get another psychiatrist to write a letter." When the reality hit her (the psychiatrist) that my mother would have three more weeks to live, she decided to write a letter. I had to push her—she didn't immediately come to my aid. I definitely had to push. I had to say—"My mother is dying, I cannot have this baby right now." The bizarre thing is that it was all because of family connections. In fact, this psychiatrist that by chance my mother had seen had also gone to medical school with an uncle of mine who was a very famous surgeon. The psychiatrist she referred me to was the psychiatrist who had counseled my uncle. I never looked at the note. The fact that he had counseled my uncle, who was suicidal—actively suicidal—gave him ample excuse to say that there was psychosis in my family. And also my mother was psychotic. Which was why the first shrink had written the note. My mother was actively psychotic. So that was very scary for me . . . it's like I had to admit I was using their craziness on some level for me to get an abortion.

So it was all set, but they couldn't schedule me for the surgery for a month or so. And in the meanwhile, my mother did die. I had the abortion, I think a week after my mother died. I was fourteen weeks pregnant by then, so I was really far along.

My mother never knew. I couldn't. . . . I told my sister, and at that point in my life, my older sister was much stronger than I was. But, still, I think she was shocked. We couldn't talk about it at all. My younger sister had been in Guatemala teaching school, and I hadn't seen her for a year and a half and she had to get on an airplane and come home to be with my mother, so it was hard to talk with her about it. My mother dying took precedence over everything. There was a close friend I was able to talk to about it. The man I was with at the time was very accepting and warm and supportive.

It felt absolutely clear to me that I had to have the abortion, but in such a way that I had to make myself much weaker than I actually was. If it was legal, I could've just gone to a clinic and finished it right then. I had to see a therapist, and I ended up being in therapy, continuing therapy afterward. What I remember thinking is, I know I'm not crazy. I'm under enormous stress. My mother's dying. I can't have a baby right now. I don't know what having a baby would do to me right now. I just know I can't handle it. I knew that, and I also knew I was not psychotic, but it was very scary to me. I'm sure that was why both psychiatrists readily agreed, "Yeah, give this lady an abortion. Her uncle tried to kill himself. Her mother had a schizophrenic break," so to them I was the next logical candidate. And on some level I felt that, too. If I had been pregnant and they hadn't been in treatment, I would have had to get an illegal abortion—but the situation couldn't have been worse, and that was why I was able to get a legal one. I was lucky. My family was crazy enough to have a shrink attached to it.

BITTER
TESTIMONY

Nora

She is a feminist historian and educator.

There was a doctor who did surgical abortions in Virginia, in the early fifties. He was ultimately arrested and, I believe, sent to prison. I remember reading about his arrest in the *Daily News*.

I went to him, to that place in Virginia, in the spring of '52. He was recommended by a doctor in Washington, D.C., who I think may have gotten a cut of the money. (He maintained that he didn't, but he talked about it so much that I think he probably did.)

Preparations for doing this were very complicated and anxiety-filled. I had to stand on a street corner in Washington, D.C., holding a copy of *Time* magazine. A woman was supposed to approach me and ask me if I had a problem, and I said, "Yes, I have a problem," and, "Can we discuss it?" She said, "No, this is only the first stage." Then I had to make a phone call and this time I was told to be in a hotel lobby with a copy of the *Washington Post*, which I thought was kind of funny, since *most* people carried the *Washington Post*. The next stage happened a week later. I was picked up by a car, on still another street corner, by someone who took me to a place where there was a long black limousine waiting. I think there were three or four other young women in the limousine when I got in. I can remember that the radio was on, and Rockefeller was trying to get the Presidential nomination, in preparation for the '52 election. By the time I got in the car, I think I figured everything was okay. In the earliest stages I was afraid of being turned down. I had some idea that I had to be the right kind of person for them to accept. It's a little weird to have thought that. . . .

All right, then we left Washington, and the car stopped, and the driver said, "And now, for fun, we're going to put these little goggles over your eyes." And so we all wore masks. But the limousine had opaque windows, so no one could see that these people were sitting there wearing masks. And then we arrived at a farmhouse. I know you'll be able to find information about this operation, but I can't tell you his name, because I never knew. When we got to the farmhouse, it was very well staffed. There were a lot of guards, strong, tough-looking men. The limousine was put in a garage and we walked from there into the house. There were guards standing around with guns, three or four nurses, and a staff of maybe ten. The procedure itself was a D&C with local anesthesia, which meant that there was not too much pain, but it was scary as hell. The woman who had met me on the corner was there as a kind of social worker, I guess, to say pleasant things. I remember she asked me who my favorite movie stars were, and I said, "Oh, Christ, leave me alone." [Laughing.] That was supposed to be . . . help!

And the doctor. I couldn't see the doctor because he was all done up for surgery. He talked as he worked, because I think he sensed that I didn't want the routine: "Who are your favorite movie stars?" So he said, "You know, the things people talk about are interesting. I have had movie stars on this table, I've had doctors, lawyers, etc. . . . etc. . . ." The doctor did have a somewhat reassuring quality. I had heard stories about people on the table being called whores and sluts by the doctors, but this man was really trying to let me know that I was being well taken care of. And then later someone said that there was a landing field there, and that they brought in helicopters and private planes.

This cost four hundred dollars. It was well done. I had volunteered to be first, not wanting to see or hear anything else, but I
found out later that I wouldn't have seen or heard anything
because there were television sets all over the house, playing
very loudly, and in addition, the toilets were calibrated to flush
every half-minute or so, so there was a lot of noise. If anyone
had freaked out and yelled, I don't think you would have heard
it. My guess was there was also a lot of soundproofing.

I just remember being terrified. When it was over, I was
taken into a bedroom and laid down with white sheets. The
nurses had white uniforms, so it was all this sterile kind of
thing, and then we were taken back to Washington—the same
routine.

The driver took each person back to where he picked them
up, and I said, "For four hundred dollars I think I should be
taken home," and he said, "But then I will know where you
live!" and I said, "And I can identify you more carefully, so let's
call it a trade." But he kept saying, "But I've never done that
before!" And I kept saying, "For four hundred dollars . . ." Finally he took me home, and that was the end of that.

I was given antibiotics and pills for breast milk. As far as I
could see, it was done very well. The whole operation must
have involved a great deal of money.

I never knew anyone else who went there. At that time I was
nineteen, and I had learned about all this in secret, and carried
it out in secret, and didn't discuss it with anyone. The only
person who knew where I was was a woman in my office. The
man I was dating did not know I was having the abortion. He
knew I was pregnant, and had wanted to get married. I was very
relieved that I had managed to get out of this mess. I had no
feelings of being guilty or having been a murderer, or . . . I had
none of that.

No later than the mid-fifties, the doctor was arrested. He
must have been involved with so many payoffs that one of them
didn't go through. There were so many people involved. Well,
four hundred dollars. I made fifty dollars a week, but I managed

it on my own. I had some savings. And I said, well, that would never happen again. Unfortunately, that wasn't true. The next time was with Dr. Spencer. You already know about him.

And the third time was a Dr. Abelove in Brooklyn. At that point I was married, and my husband was insistent that we were not ready to have a child. Abelove was a G.P., I think, with a private practice in the basement of a building in a residential area. I don't remember who had told me about him, but I know several people who had gone to him, and he seemed pleasant enough. However, there was a great problem that developed. He told me that if I could be hypnotized, he could do the abortion without using any injections or medication, and it would be a lot easier. And so when I went to him for the preliminary interview, he tried hypnosis, and it worked like a charm. I couldn't raise my arm, I couldn't blink my eye, so, terrific, that's what it was going to be. Well, what had worked for the practice session did not work for the real thing . . . and it was quite horrendous. He was very . . . I can remember the sweat pouring down his face, and him saying, "Holy shit, what am I going to do?" I was in terrible pain, and I just . . . I . . . He kept saying he couldn't stop, and I called him a fuckin' butcher, and we exchanged a few words there, and he kept saying, "I'm so sorry I let you do it" . . . he didn't know I had ambivalence about it, which I certainly did.

Everything seemed okay. He talked to my husband when he was finished, and he gave us the whole thing about if there are cramps or hemorrhaging, I was to come back to him. But he kept wiping his brow, as if I had caused him terrible problems, you see, and saying, "I'll never do this again unless I'm really sure."

Well, what I discovered during the next three or four years, when I tried to have a baby, was that during that process, my cervix was lacerated, and I consequently had two late miscarriages, and ultimately I had to have a corrective operation. I gather that the chance of lacerating the cervix are nine out of ten when you're dealing with a moving body. I doubt that he knew he'd done that, because the doctors who examined me afterward saw nothing wrong. It was only empirically, when I later became pregnant and the fetus reached the fifth month the first time, and the fourth month the second time—when the fetus reached a certain size—the cervix was too elastic, and I went into labor. It took some time to discover that.

I'm resentful about the whole experience, but I don't know who to be angry at: Abelove, my husband, me for being too passive. In the meantime, I helped quite a number of other women to locate help, and I heard about many others.

I took someone to a doctor on Long Island named Lothringer. Does that sound familiar? It was in *The New York Times*. Remember that? This was the one who did an abortion on someone who was five and a half months pregnant and she died on the operating table, he chopped her up into little pieces and flushed her down his toilet. Let's see. He was arrested in the summer of 1961. He came to trial during the great newspaper strike in New York which lasted for nine months. There was no real coverage. I looked at *Time* and *Life* and in the Long Island papers, and they had a file on him, but it wasn't as much as there would have been.

My friend wanted me to go with her because she was very frightened. She had gotten his name from someplace and she wanted me to check out whether he was reliable and competent. He had an office on a boulevard in Queens and he was a G.P. I remember he had NO SMOKING signs all over, which was very unusual in the sixties, and while I was waiting, a child rushed in from the street with a bloody finger and was yelling, "Doctor, Doctor, help me," and the doctor was very sweet and put him on his lap and put a Band-Aid on.

Anyway, then I went in to find out what he did, and in retrospect, I should never have let my friend go there, but . . . He wanted to show me his tools, his equipment. He'd gotten his instruments from West Germany, he said, and they were the only instruments that were safe to use. I still think of it as tools—and he started talking about the price.

I had been told it was four hundred dollars. Somehow there was this magic figure of four hundred dollars. I had been told that this guy charged four hundred dollars so I had four hundred dollars in cash. He asked me how much I had brought. I said, "What do you mean how much did I bring?" I said, "What is the price?" and he said, "What did you bring?" We did that for a while, and then he took out a piece of paper and said, "Let's play a game. You write on your piece of paper what you have and I'll write on my piece of paper what I want," and I got up and said, "This is beginning to sound very ugly. I think we'd better forget the whole thing." At that point he said, "Are you willing to pay four hundred dollars?" and I said, "Yes."

Well, look, everything seemed very clean, and he had all the medical degrees on the wall, but his showing me the instruments was weird. So he told me to go away, and to come back and get my friend later, she would be fine, and she was. She didn't like him. She said he made a comment—he told her to pull her slip up, and when she hesitated he said, "Well, you've done that many times in the past," or some such innuendo. She didn't like him, but she had no problem. He had used a local anesthetic so she didn't have much pain and she was fine.

It was maybe two weeks to a month later, she phoned me at work. She started to scream; I thought she'd had some kind of breakdown. She said, "Go get the newspaper!" So indeed I went out, and the newsstand people were yelling, "Dismembered body found on Long Island," and I knew in a minute that was Dr. Lothringer. Later at his trial, friends, neighbors, patients came in and said what a wonderful man he was and that he'd been a bulwark in the community, and if he had done this they thought it was just a fluke. They seemed to want to excuse him. What he had done was—the parents of a very young girl, a convent student, had come to him, and he had said that she was too advanced. And then they came back and offered more money and he had said okay. Well, as I understand it, you can't do an abortion at that stage, so she died, and he did what I said—chopped her up and put her in the toilet. Then—get this—he decided that his goose was cooked, so he and his nurse, who was apparently his mistress, took off for Switzerland. He'd had these plans—Swiss accounts and all kinds of arrangements in case this happened. They went to the airport, and he made a phone call to some kind of company—what we call it is Roto-Rooter—the folks that clean out drains. He called and told them he was leaving the country, but that he had noticed that his toilet seemed to be clogged, and would they mind pumping it out and that he would send them a check. So he got on the plane, and they came, but someone noticed a—you can imagine—something surfacing.

Now, question: Was that his way of confessing, or did he really imagine their equipment was such that they could get rid of it? I suppose we'll never know that, right? It sort of looked like a confession. So that's what he did, and then the parents came forward and said their daughter was missing—well, they found her, right?

He then was "on the lam" till they found him the next spring. They found him in Switzerland and he was extradited and brought back. I do not know what kind of sentence he got, because I only saw one little thing from—maybe it was *Newsday*.

The woman whom I'd taken took the approach that I had done something wrong by taking her there, and I must confess, I got very rattled by the whole thing and had to pull myself together to realize that, no, I had not done anything wrong. However, I did rework that scene with the tools and thought that I perhaps should have been suspicious, but . . . let us say that was my last mission of charity. I never did it again. It really, really unnerved me. I went through the conversation, the way the office looked, I even spoke to a therapist about it. I finally decided that I did do what she asked me to do. It wasn't as if I had walked into the stereotypically dirty, awful place, you know, it wasn't like that.

Before that, I took a friend to one other place. I went with a Black friend to a woman in Harlem, whose name was Lassiter.

Mrs. Lassiter seemed to be really well known. She had been a practical nurse, perhaps, I think not an R.N. She had a very dark apartment which may have been clean, but you couldn't tell because it was so dark, with lots of Jesus pictures. The walls were covered. It had the feeling of a lot of satin, a lot of net, and a lot of Jesus stuff. What she did was insert a catheter and what you were supposed to do was go away and later cramp and expel it, and that's what happened to this woman. It took a few days. She went again later, to Lassiter.

The woman was very sweet, I remember. It seems to me there was a lot of religious talk. She was a lot cheaper, maybe one hundred fifty dollars, something like that. She seemed to come out of the midwife tradition. I had a sense that she felt she was doing something useful. I believe that there was some necessity for personal references to go to her. I don't think you could just call her up.

You always hear horror stories about the dirt: dirty fingernails, instruments that were not sterilized, but I think sometimes the horror had to do with other things.

I think for many people the illegality was very frightening, not only in the sense of what the punishment might be if you were caught. It seems to me that any woman would feel a lot of fear about the possibility of the operation being stopped in the middle. That is a very ghastly thought. That was my case with Abelove. He said, "I can't stop, there's too much bleeding, I can't stop." Now, I don't know why he couldn't stop, but there was always that possibility that while the person is doing that to you, that in come the cops, right? Those are the newspaper accounts. I have a feeling that if you find the newspaper articles about the doctor in Virginia, it's going to turn out that the police came in when a patient was on the table. That's catching them red-handed, the way the cops want it, right?

The minute I had one experience with illegal abortion, I knew it had to be legalized. That's why I'm sitting here telling you thirty-five years later. I tell my students constantly that all they have to do is know what it was like—and they'd better get on the bus, they'd better get to Washington. But it's hard, because they really have trouble understanding. The word has to be spread. I teach a Women's Studies course and I always tell them an anecdote or two, sort of an amalgam of the things I've told you, but without identifying myself as a patient. I show them copies of a letter Dr. Spencer wrote to me. I have a copy for you. I'm sorry I don't still have the original. The signature is not very clear on this copy, but you can just imagine this dear man sitting down at his typewriter and typing this out, in his very own, very funny typing. Of course, this indicates that he was still trying to help. It still comes through in this letter how concerned he was about the women he couldn't help, because he wasn't able to perform the abortion himself at the time. [She offers the following letter, reproduced here with spelling and grammatical errors intact.]

March 19, 1959

Call Dr. Eduardo Elias 7-6546, 1070 San Migual St. Havana Cuba, ask for an appointment, but do not give your real name. When you arrive in Havana go to the FLAMINGO Hotel, and ask for a $7 room. When the appointment hour arrives, walk to the Drs. Office, and make sure you have not eaten, or drank anything for the four previous hrs. When you arrive at the Drs. office make sure you enter the Bldg. that has the Drs. Name upon it as well as the No. 1070. When you enter the Dr. will show his Medical Papers, they contain his name, his address and Photo, so in this manner you can be positive you are with the correct M.D. Dr. Elias will charge $50 if under 3 months, $200 when past this mark, Time Limit 4.5 Mo, and at this time may charge more. Your round trip from N.Y.C. by air $155. Food Taxi. $15. Down one day and back the next, work the following day. IN CUBA THIS OPERATION IS A RACKET, that is why you give false name, as the Police take all calls, and they are in the racket. Never be surprised if some stranger should call you by name, and say, "Follow me and I'll take you to Dr. Elias. This is a method used so you would not see him. Tell such a party you are not a patient. So many persons come to the Island for the operation, that if residents think that is why you came, they may try to take you to some one who does this work and receive a bonus. And they may take you to a party not an M. D. Dr. Elias is very reliable, he speaks Spanish, but understands English if you speak slowly. You see him and I am positive your problem will be solved in a most satisfactory manner. FOLLOW ORDERS AND YOU WILL HAVE NO TROUBLE.

I know my students tell a couple other people, but it's sort of, so what. And I also tell them that their mothers know about this too, and that their mothers are not going to tell them, but their mothers do know. Many of them come to me and tell me that yes, their mothers did know about all this, and I tell them it's unlikely their mothers will ever tell them what happened to them, but I'll bet they'll talk about a friend. I think it's interesting for the students. It opens up a different kind of relationship, to think that their mothers knew about sexuality at that time.

It's not that I'm trying to get them to find out their mother's secrets, it's not like that, but in times of witch hunts or sexual repression, when people talk about events, they always talk about *other* people. That's a kind of code that you must understand.

I tell them about Spencer, and how he was the one ray of hope.

In our community, there's a very organized anti-abortion group that pickets and does what they call "sidewalk counseling": they grab women and show them pictures of bloody fetuses and all that stuff. So our people formed an escort service to help these women get into the clinic. You know, just to say, "You don't have to listen. Do you want to walk in?" etc. I mention only once to students that if they have time to do that just once,

it would be very revelatory for them to realize the intensity of
the feeling to delegalize abortion. Those people are zealots.
They are totally committed. The ones in our area are not dangerous in a physical sense, but there have been bomb threats
written by local cuckoos. That's always the danger. The particular people I know—I know who they are—spend their time,
it would seem, praying and picketing. They are determined to
stay until the clinic is closed. You know their wonderful man
who wrote the book, 99 *Ways to Close an Abortion Clinic*. He
came, and was quoted as saying he never advocates bombings,
but if one occurs, he doesn't lose any sleep over it!

He also made a comment that I was very grateful for his
having made. He said that the reason he hates feminists is that
they want to be like men and not *have* to get pregnant. And you
see, in a way he's right. That *is* what we want. I didn't hear him
while he was there, but we were getting crazy calls in the office,
and the police were very concerned. Fortunately, nothing terrible happened.

Are you going to do any background about the nineteenth
century when abortion was not illegal? You know Linda Gordon's book, *Women's Body, Women's Right?* That's really the
source. It's the history of the birth control movement, and
there's stuff about the nineteenth century, when it was legal.
Even the Catholic Church accepted abortions in the first trimester, or until "quickening." Not only was it not illegal, but
abortions were advertised. In newspapers there would be tiny
little notices in, like, the *New York Review* saying So-and-so can
help you with your problem. They would do that. They were
probably midwives, and in those days they would advertise pills,
which probably were ergot, ergotrate of some kind, and they
would say that these were for "better health and a sense of well-
being," and also they would say in big face: "Do not take them
if you are pregnant because they will cause you to miscarry.
WARNING: DO NOT TAKE THESE." Imagine: A hundred years
ago they were advertised openly, not in sleazy underground
journals.

Max

Max is an artist who earns his living as a carpenter. Twenty years ago, two women he was with had abortions. Now he is struggling to understand how women feel. He feels he was insensitive as a young man, but that he "pretty much handled this the way most guys would have." After all, he says, "I was dealing with the whole bill of goods that I grew up with in the fifties."

Well, my first experience was with my first girlfriend in college. We had been seeing each other for about one year. We were having relations and obviously, at that time not too much effort was made to use contraception. The reality of actually having a baby and being responsible about contraception never really made that much of an impression on me. So, she went away for the summer vacation. When school started again in September she came back and the first thing she said was that she hadn't had her period. For nearly two months she hadn't checked to see what was up. As far as any kind of immediate feelings, it didn't register on any heavy level. I didn't think—Oh my God, I have to marry this woman or—Oh my God, what are we gonna do; none of that. I was just having a wait-and-see attitude. Well, her period didn't come and then a little tension started to build and we had to seriously start considering what we were gonna do. The first thing she did was go to a local doctor on the campus to find out if she was pregnant, and it turned out that she was. We didn't consider getting married. I don't think we even discussed it. At the time, I felt as though I was totally unprepared to get married. I still felt very much like a kid and she possibly felt the same way. We were in our second year of college and we wanted to finish, so we had to figure out what to do. And I guess the first thing you did in those days was to start asking friends. You know, start making phone calls and asking if anyone had an abortion, or this and that. I think a friend of ours had a girlfriend who got hold of some pills that were supposed to induce something. She gave us the phone number to get hold of this doctor. There was all kinds of intrigue and secrecy involved. It was a very hard thing to do, and to me it seemed like we weren't ever gonna pull it off. It just seemed like the way it was happening, there was some possibility that we might have been ripped off; getting sugar pills or something.

Meanwhile, time was going by. She went back to the doctor who had diagnosed the pregnancy, and I think she might have even asked him if he would give her an abortion. He was very nervous and upset about it. He said, "I can't do that. I can't legally give you an abortion," and I think he gave her a shot of something. He might have actually given her a saline solution injection or something like that to induce miscarriage, because after she left him and she came home that night, she had a miscarriage. So that was the end of it. You know, "Whew! That's the end of that!"

The second one wasn't as fortunate. I was with somebody else and it was the same sort of thing. I was basically not careful about contraception and she got pregnant. I guess I was around twenty or twenty-two, and we knew more people that had abortions by then. You know, a few more years down the pike, a few more connections. I was actually living with her sister and brother-in-law. I was a lot closer to her sister than to her. She was a kid—a sudden fling; it was pretty rotten. I felt bad about the whole thing. She had just left home and I was just pretty much out having a good time, and I wasn't really thinking about anything as far as a long-term relationship, and she was very young. I had much more in common with her sister; and here her sister and I were planning this whole thing—what to do about the fact that she was pregnant, which caused her to be very upset. She felt like she was being manipulated, like nobody even asked her how she felt about the whole thing. It was all up to the older people. That's the way it was; nobody's getting married here, I mean it was like, uh, no thought of that, she just had to have the abortion. Her sister found out about a doctor somewhere in Queens that did abortions.

We had broken up at the end of the summer and it was after that she found out that she was pregnant, so it made it bad 'cause we had to get back together just to discusss what we had to do about it. The doctor charged one thousand dollars for the abortion. I didn't have any money at the time—I wasn't making very much and I didn't have anything saved. So I asked some friends for some loans, and I came back and gave her sister the cash. I don't think I had much to do with my ex-girlfriend anymore because as I said, there was a strain because we had broken up and she really didn't want to deal with it or me. I pretty much had to go through her sister to arrange everything. I just gave her the thousand dollars and left. That was it. I didn't have any more to do with it. She and her sister went to the place. She was nervous and the doctor was very brusque and he seemed very nervous and on edge and, uh, and he asked for the money first before he did the abortion and he wasn't at all consoling in any way. All he wanted to do was get it over with and get her out of there as fast as he could. So it was a very bad experience for her. It left a lot of bitter feelings. The whole experience did. Number one, the fact that we had split up and she was pregnant, and then I had sort of—she was put aside when her sister and I decided what to do about her. Just having to go through the abortion itself was a bad experience for her, and the way the doctor treated her . . .

I don't know what I would have done if an abortion had not been available. I suppose in the first case, we might have gotten married because we loved each other. If there was absolutely no way, and she was going to have a baby, I don't think I would have just split. But the second one, due to the fact that it was a very short relationship, and we had broken up, and then she became pregnant, I certainly don't think I would have gotten married. Exactly what I would have done, I don't know. Offhand I can't think of another friend of mine who had to do that. It is surprising because it seems that it could happen a lot. It seems as though I would always hear from women who had abortions, but I'd never hear from any guys that they were involved in any way. At the time, I did very little, considering the fact that there was a baby growing.

I pretty much was dealing with the whole bill of goods that I grew up with in the fifties—what a man's responsibility was and what a woman's responsibility was—the options that you do have when you come up with a situation where someone gets pregnant. As far as a moral issue, people shouldn't be doing something illegal, but I think I pretty much handled this the way most guys would have. I would say, oh, that if I had the same situation today, the only thing that really has changed is that abortions are readily available. I would still deal with the same emotional things. This woman is pregnant! What am I going to do? We have basically the same options, have an abortion; get married; the same pressures are on you. Certainly, if you could prevent pregnancy, that would be the way to go.

My sister had to get married. It wasn't a shock, and it didn't even mean that she was pregnant. The parents just found out that she was having sex and that was enough. My mother found her birth control pills in the suitcase when she came home from college. They really put the screws through her. That was the same time I was having the problem with the second time, you know, so I couldn't support her too much. My father cried, "My daughter's having sex!" My mother gave like this virgin angel act: "We gotta call him up and nail him down and you're gonna get married now or you're not gonna see him anymore." It cast a pall on the whole marriage. It's as if she was pregnant. A few people went to the reception, but she couldn't wear a white gown. It was like the Dark Ages in the sixties. . . .

Lydia

An intense, outspoken political activist, Lydia points out implications of illegal abortion that go beyond the obvious.

I think it was about 1963, the year after the Cuban missile crisis. I became pregnant and decided to have the baby. I was working as an au pair in Sicily. I was twenty-two or twenty-three. It didn't work—I miscarried, and I needed to see a doctor because the bleeding didn't stop. I got into a whole situation of being in a country where none of these things are acknowledged at all, and could find no doctor who was willing to treat a woman for this sort of thing if she was unmarried. And after many inquiries, including the U.S. Embassy—I really tried everything—I finally found a doctor who seemed very intelligent and understanding, who agreed to see me privately in his office after hours, for a D&C. In the middle of it, it was very scary, because the nurse suddenly noticed I wasn't wearing a wedding ring, and the doctor assured her, saying, no, I was married, I was married, and my husband was outside waiting for me. But there were a lot of potential legal complications there, and the family I was staying with felt that they could be threatened by the police if anybody found out about it. In fact the police did not catch on to the story, and nothing happened, but the people I was staying with felt a little used, because they didn't believe that this miscarriage was involuntary. They thought that I was so young, it was perfectly normal that I wouldn't want to have

the baby. They thought it could have been arranged more tact-
fully if I really wanted to end the pregnancy. And I kept saying,
"No, no, it's not like that."

So, you see, the problem is that anywhere abortion is illegal,
any woman who has a miscarriage can be suspected of an il-
legally self-inflicted abortion. And that affects the entire medical care of women who are pregnant if abortion is criminal;
doctors are subject to legal prosecution themselves, and so they
become paranoid. And if doctors are affected, women are affected, especially those who are unmarried.

This happened to my stepmother when abortion was illegal.
She had been very brutally raped and beaten, and she went to a
doctor, wearing dark glasses, accompanied by my father. She
was trying to get medical care because she was afraid that maybe
this guy had been sick, and she wanted to get antibiotics or
something. And she could get no treatment at all. This was in
New York City around the same period, in the early sixties.
Even though she was accompanied by her legal husband and
was black and blue, she could get no help whatsoever.

I don't think she went to the police. In those days it meant a
lot to go to the police, and she had probably been advised not
to. It would have been even more traumatizing, even more of a
violation, and I think she felt that it probably would not have
resulted in catching the guy. Well, she couldn't get help, she
realized, because the doctors thought that she was trying to get
an abortion, and that she would go so far as to get herself beaten
up and come in with her husband. So, you see, it's not just the
major, very, very important issues, but it would affect a lot
more people in subtle ways.

Doctors were approached by women who induced bleeding
and then came to the doctor for a D&C, hoping that the pregnancy was past saving. They had to look for this in each case
and ferret out these "criminal intentions." So, we must consider
that if abortion were made illegal, even the good doctors, even
the sensitive ones, would be put under pressure.

Wilfredo

"It's easy to find the underground when you're living in the ghetto."

Wilfredo's story appears here because his wife suggested during her interview that he would have a unique point of view. Although he doubts that his stories will be "anything unusual," he has agreed to be interviewed too.

Wilfredo grew up in the Puerto Rican ghetto. He is a wiry, intense, dark-haired man in his thirties. Although distance and time have modulated his style, his quick and agile movements and the echo of Latin rhythms as he speaks take you back to New York's Lower East Side.

As his story unfolds, he remembers more and more, until he finally uncovers the story closest to him.

Well, it was supposed to be a séance, and I used to go because I knew the family, and my mother used to go, so she would drag me along. They'd have like good séances and bad séances, where you'd go to a good spiritualist and whatever she did was for the good, and then there was the bad spiritualist, so if you wanted to get back at somebody or do something evil you'd go to this one. I didn't believe in it too much, but sometimes the things seemed very real, and some of the predictions, for some reason would turn out to be true, but I used to laugh a lot, and they'd pick me out of the audience and say, "And *you*, you have an evil spirit who thinks this is a big joke." That's what they told me, and I used to just laugh some more about that.

In terms of pregnancy, they would combine an abortion with the séance, in conjunction with spiritualism. I remember one time they had candles lit and it was just like a regular séance, like they were praying to God.

They would make the person appear to be very comfortable, I don't know how, with all those candles and chants, maybe like hypnotizing her. They were chanting and they would have incense burning, and they would do a real big number, calling in the spirits to help and to make sure that everything went right: using black magic to do good, so to speak. They did induce a trance in the person. I was around to see that, but I didn't stick around to see the rest because they were going to perform it there and . . . uh . . . the method was lye in a douche bag and they had some long implements. I knew that the lye they were using was a Drano-type thing. It was for cleaning drains—toilet and sink drains. I knew that had to be harmful, but they used it. They said it would induce abortion. Of course something like that would induce an abortion—but what else would it do? I remember them rubbing some ointment on her belly. At that point, I decided that these people were crazy and I didn't want to see.

I didn't know the girl personally. I had seen her around, and I knew she didn't want to have the baby because she didn't want her mom to know. Back then she couldn't go to a doctor, and even if she could she didn't have the money and she was under-age, so they had to do it this way, and you know, they felt that the best way to do it was to go to someone who does séances and who is in tune with, like the spirits and God. You know, in the city whatever they pick up in life, like going to a séance instead of going to a hospital, it kind of goes on down the family line. So they said it was the best way because these people knew what they were doing, but where did they come off using lye? Have you ever heard of this before?

It took about a week. The girl had to hang out there for a couple of days before they let her go home, and what she had was a partial abortion. They thought everything was fine and it was all over with, but the girl ended up going to the hospital afterward because she got burned inside from the lye.

Obviously, when the women were taken to the hospital, the doctors would know, because they would find a substance in their bodies, but the extent of where, who, when . . . nobody ever knew. I had heard of other stories like this before. One woman—and I knew her—had this done to her, the same method, but she was not okay. She ended up going to the hospital. After that she just could have no more children. Things like that, it was pretty common. It was a regular practice. The ones that were involved in evil black magic could use it to do good, because they were tuned in to spirits, and if you wanted an abortion, they were the experts. Meanwhile they couldn't do it without lye and those long implements that they used. And that's the way they did abortions, with spiritualism. . . .

This was in Manhattan, 13th Street and Avenue B, in that general area. It's easy to find the underground when you live in the ghetto. In some places they did have underground doctors, I remember, and those were where most of the women wanted to go because they felt safer. Now, whether the doctor was a real doctor or just a dropout from medical school, no one really knew. I remember there were a few buildings that had doctors that would perform underground abortions, and some of them were even made up to be like legitimate clinics where they would take care of other medical needs, but abortions would be their main business. And usually it was young girls, young frightened girls who had nowhere to turn. Mom's not supposed to know she was fooling around and got pregnant, so what can she do? She sells some drugs to get enough money to try to have an illegal abortion. I used to hang out in the streets a lot, and I remember being out in the street and seeing the ambulance pull up. They would take these girls to the hospital. It was pretty common at the time, in the sixties when I was growing up. Especially for young girls. What else could they do?

Some of the girls knew that they were babies themselves and that they shouldn't have a child. There's a thing in the city where women—young girls—tend to follow a trend, and it's the thing for them to have babies, because there's nothing else but having a child and going on welfare. This way, if you have children, then you've accomplished something in life and now you are a mother. But some of the young girls realized that if they had children they were going to be in a lot of trouble and they couldn't in any way bring up a child. And some of the girls—actually they were young teenagers—who couldn't have abortions, sometimes they ended up abandoning their children on the street.

I remember, my mom and I once found a baby in the garbage can, crying. A little infant, right in front of our house. I couldn't believe it. We all heard this noise, and we walked right to where it was in the garbage can, wrapped up in a blanket, a baby. Young girls, if they can't have abortions they will give it up, or else they will just get rid of it. They're frightened, they don't know what to do. I knew this one girl. We used to go to her house a lot for séances, and she stayed over at my house one time, and I knew she was pregnant because she told me she felt like she was, but she was afraid to tell her mom. But she did tell her after all, and her mom took care of it for her. They're Catholic, and she wasn't married, and the man was unacceptable, and the hospital didn't perform it, so her mom would do it, because her mom was like a midwife. I just thought it was bizarre how these people would think that they knew how to perform abortions with coat hangers and lye. I couldn't understand that.

Oh! . . . I remember another girl! She was my girlfriend! She was my first love. Yes, Rosa. I was somewhere around fourteen or fifteen. She was about the same age. It was funny. When I was a kid, we were able to get involved with a girl even at thirteen or fourteen, and sometimes the parents would think that was better than having us running around in the street.

Rosa . . . Rosa and I were together for quite some time, for several years when we were kids. We slept together, at my mom's or at her mom's, and they accepted that. They didn't care—they figured it was the best thing, but she got pregnant.

She had something done to her, and after it was done, nothing happened. They had said everything was fine and she should wait a few days. Two days later she came over to my house and said, "Wilfredo, take me to the hospital!" She was bleeding. And sure enough the hospital said she was having a miscarriage and it was due to having an abortion done on her that didn't take.

She didn't tell me until we were on the way to the hospital that it was due to the fact that she had that illegal abortion and they told her to wait a few days and not to worry. How crazy! Wait a couple of days.

I was a kid. I didn't know much. There was no talk about birth control, or sex. No.

Rosa never got pregnant from me after that, for all the years we were together. She always wanted to have a baby, ever since she was a kid, so she would be a mother, she would be accepted, so she would be worth something. Yes, Rosa had that too. I remember.

It was very hush-hush. It's funny how young kids, like my girlfriend and myself, no one has to tell you not to go out there and talk about this. For some reason you know that you don't go out there and talk about this on the street—you don't report this. You don't have to be told, you just know this. So we all knew it, and we never said anything to anybody about it. And we were in a community where it's common practice to keep your mouth shut about everything that's illegal.

EASING
THE BURDEN

THE DOCTORS

Ed

There is a gleam and a twinkle in his eyes, and if you didn't know he was a psychiatrist, you might think he was a seasoned Irish seaman.

He packs his pipe slowly as he begins to talk.

Now, there was a period of time when the hospital policy was that women could have their pregnancies terminated after a review by the board. Someone created a mechanism so that there were not great risks to any of the physicians involved. I never ran into any conflicts or resistance to what I was doing. Nobody ever said anything to me, outwardly, and I never picked up any hint of anything, and I don't know that it affected my practice, or my sources of referral. . . . Nobody ever said anything. Of course, this was all open and aboveboard. It was not criminal. Somebody made the effort to make this possible, and my guess is that these were prestigious physicians on the board of the hospital who must have had a part in creating this process.

The way people would come to me would be that their obstetrician would be building a case to present to the board which included some psychiatric evaluation. The hidden message to me would be: Please find that this lady is in serious danger of suicide or something like this, so that I can get permission from the board to terminate the pregnancy.

There seemed to be several obstetricians and gynecologists who were interested in doing this sort of thing, and since I was on the staff of the hospital, they would refer patients to me. There were other psychiatrists, I understand, who did not like doing this kind of consultation. I was happy to be of help. What I wasn't happy about sometimes was the idea of stretching the point of seriousness, because statistically, you know, there was much less risk that a pregnant woman would kill herself. Unmarried women who were pregnant did not commit suicide as much as women who were not pregnant, so I knew I was stretching the truth, but somehow the people I interviewed always managed to say that they were so desperate that they would kill themselves if they didn't get this procedure, so that is what I would say in the letter, and that's how it would happen.

The people who came to me included fifteen-year-old girls, an unmarried woman in her late thirties and just about everyone in between. There were married women who knew that their families were as much as they could manage, and that their birth control techniques had failed, and that they had to do something else, and I certainly agreed with them. As a matter of fact, I think that the bulk of them—and I want to get out these records and give them to you, because I think that by going over the records we can reconstruct the figures about them—the most common thing was a woman with two children, and birth control had failed. It wasn't as if these people had been out fooling around and had gotten impregnated by somebody other than their husband. It was nothing like that.

I wasn't seeing call girls, I wasn't seeing hookers. I wasn't seeing promiscuous people. I was seeing ordinary people who maybe on some occasion had committed an indiscretion, but for the most part were part of a loving couple that just couldn't sustain the idea of having another child. And the idea that they should be put through this process seemed pretty awful, and I didn't want to make life any more complicated for them. I tried to make the interviews as supportive of their decision as I possibly could. After all, I wasn't directing them, I was just supporting a determination that they had already arrived at. I really didn't like the process. Interestingly, none of these people ever returned for any kind of follow-up. Maybe it's because their problem was solved. I never saw any of them again.

I remember a tiny little girl, about fifteen, who was brought by her parents. This was a very responsible, community-based family. Both the parents had careers. Somehow the girl got herself pregnant, and I'm not even sure she knew how. She certainly didn't know why. She was almost mute. . . . I had to coax her a little bit to get her to say the magic words that would allow me to report to her obstetrician that she was in serious danger if the pregnancy was continued. There was no question about the validity of the process. She certainly should not have been forced to continue this pregnancy. She was really a very passive, helpless little girl. I remember that very well.

In my work, I ran a residential treatment program for adolescent girls for a while. The kids that I was working with, or trying to work with, were for the most part unwanted children. They were unwanted children, and they had been thrown away. They were abandoned. I was working with Black Protestant young girls and women, age thirteen to twenty or so. A typical story was that of a girl who was born in the South to a teenage mother. The mother went North to establish herself, and the child stayed with the grandparents. Then when the child got to be a teenager, she was sent to New York City. She reentered the life of her mother, who had mixed feelings about this. The girl had to deal with the culture shock of coming from the rural South to urban New York City, and the mother's ambivalence, and then the difficulties began. The mother had a boyfriend who started fooling around with the girl, and the mother didn't want to believe it, so she got a petition to say the girl was incorrigible, and had her placed. The kid would say to me, "I was the one who got messed around, I was the one who got raped, and I got put away." Where's the justice there?

I became more and more aware that unwanted children, unplanned-for children, should not be imposed upon unwilling parents, for anybody's sake, particularly for the kid's sake.

And to say that there are adoptive people out there who are

just eager to have these children, well, sure, if they are blond, blue-eyed little girls of documented genetic heritage, well, that may be true, but that isn't true for a Black kid. That isn't true for a lot of kids. And the process is so goddamn slow that by the time it actually takes place, they are already damaged individuals.

You asked me a question that I haven't really answered for myself, and that is, "Why did I keep all the records from those cases all these years?" I don't believe very much in the ability to perceive the future, and I think there are many coincidences in life, but I don't know, I just thought that this was too valuable a bunch of stuff to just discard. I didn't know what use it would have. It had some sort of use to me, I think that it may have something to do with the struggle to understand religion, and my own heritage. I don't know, maybe I knew somehow it would be of use to somebody someday. Maybe I knew you'd come for it. . . . [Smile.]

Dr. White

His medical practice has spanned more than forty years.

He was introduced to me as a doctor with a reputation for being a strong pro-choice advocate. I was invited to his home to hear stories about the early years of his practice, when abortion was illegal. Dr. White felt a genuine concern for the women who came to him with the dilemma of unwanted pregnancy. He knew there were ways within the realm of his practice to help them, and he did.

Early on in my practice, a friend's sister found out she was pregnant. At the time she was unmarried, in her mid-thirties, and already had two children. She became so desperate that she jumped in front of a subway train at Forty-second Street and Broadway in an effort to commit suicide. She survived the accident with a fractured skull, fractured shoulder bones, and fractured pelvis, and spent four months in the hospital. Her child was delivered about three months later—a perfectly normal child. I thought if a woman was willing to go to that length to avoid a pregnancy she didn't want, then something really ought to be done, and I became an active advocate of abortion from that time on.

After that, when a woman came to me for help, and she was a patient I knew, I would be willing to go out on a limb. What I did was to examine her and try to initiate bleeding. This was done by gently introducing the instrument which I would normally use for taking endometrial biopsies. And then after starting a little bleeding I'd tell her to go home and call me back within twenty-four hours to let me know if the bleeding continued. If it did, which I expected that it would, I would then admit her as a threatened abortion and complete the process in a legitimate way. In reality, I was performing an illegal abortion. But it was under controlled circumstances, in a hospital with proper backup, anesthesia, and so forth. There were a number of instances where I thought that if some smart pathologist picked up the fact that this tissue was fairly normal, I might be asked why I did the curettage. But I was lucky. I was never questioned. And, of course, I didn't do it so frequently that there'd be a suspicion that I was practicing illegal abortion.

Now as I am talking, I recall what happened to me when I was an intern. I was very much in love with a nurse, and she became pregnant. And when it happened, we looked at each other and I said, "This can't be, I'm earning twelve dollars a month." She was doing a little better—something like fifty or seventy-five a month. And we agreed that we should have an elective abortion. I was referred to a doctor whose office was on West End Avenue, and I remember to this day—that was 1940, the summer of 1940—going to West End Avenue, on the subway from Brooklyn where we both were working. We walked into this office on West End Avenue and an older gentleman, surely in his sixties at the time, greeted us, took my nurse friend into the office. I sat in the waiting room like any other anxious partner. About an hour later, he came out and showed me the curettage, because I was a young doctor, and told me that there were twins there, and that was why he had a more difficult time than usual. He said that she would be all right, and I could take her home. I shall never forget that ride on the subway going back to Brooklyn, because of my concern that she might have been harmed in some way. She was feeling kind of beat from the ether, and she was obviously exhausted and upset by the whole experience. And that personal experience was enough to make me think women shouldn't have to carry children they don't want. . . . I think, in retrospect, we were fortunate.

Dr. Joan

During most of her thirty-seven years of medical practice, Dr. Joan has been involved in women's health care. She is steadfast in her belief that women must receive high-quality, nonjudgmental medical treatment.

You have to think of me in terms of the fact that I was born in 1926. I will be seventy-four in the year 2000, and I hope I live to be a really old lady with all my nuts and bolts upstairs, because I think it's a fabulous century. One of the advantages of aging is that you've lived through more history, so you can have much more historical perspective.

I've always been a history buff. I think it's very interesting to look at the twentieth century and look forward and think, What are future historians going to write about this century? I think one of the things will be the Women's Movement. The changes and the options for women in this century. Certainly the whole abortion rights issue is intimately tied to where women are at. I think about it a lot now because of what seems to be a swing to the right—a conservative swing. What does this mean to women? Have we really made some progress? I think for me to tell my stories about my experience as a woman physician, you have to put me in the context of women physicians of my era. You need to hear about the context so you understand my reactions, you know. You have to understand what I was like at twenty-four—a young woman physician.

Both my parents were terribly ambitious. They only had two children and they saw the American Dream as education, you know, as everything. So my brother and I were the raw material of the next generation. Luckily, we were reasonably intelligent kids so we could respond to this tremendous push. My father was a physician and my mother was a nurse. And the message from my mother—not articulated but very clear—was "Don't be a nurse, be a doctor."

I graduated from high school in 1944. We got caught in the Second World War. My brother was just a little bit older. He got caught up in the Navy and was sent to medical school. I was right behind him and went right off to medical school too. I'd been in this class of fifty-six students in my medical school, only four of us women. We were very quiet. We were so glad to be there that we were quiet, like little mice.

We let things happen that we never would today. I struggled for years, like many of us did, with "little girls are quiet." Nice women are quiet, pleasant, passive, not assertive—how I ever dealt with that message (from my mother), and yet went ahead to be on the front line of a professional career! I think I showed the strain. I had tremendous anxieties that I didn't understand. I was always afraid. I really knew very little about the social parts of life or the politics of medicine.

When I was twenty-four, an intern in Rochester, New York, I rode the ambulance. In those days we did rotating internships, which means you got assigned for six-week periods to various things: pediatrics, obstetrics, surgery. And one of my first assignments was to ride the ambulance.

I can still see this ambulance. It was sort of an old Buick-Cadillac. It looked like a hearse. It was painted white, and it had this stretcherlike thing that you stuck in the back. So unlike today's emergency rescue vehicles that have all kinds of wonderful equipment. It had this terrible siren. And these two guys—they were nineteen or twenty years old—who drove the ambulance. They were out for kicks and excitement. This was a job they liked 'cause there was always blood and gore and you never knew what was gonna happen. The three of us would sit in the front seat of the ambulance. It was always nerve-racking 'cause you never knew. . . .

So here I was, this sort of intellectual middle-class twenty-four-year-old woman. I had a little black bag with some basic medication. I have vivid memories of driving in this ambulance all over the city of Rochester, at any time, day or night. We'd be on for twelve hours and off for twelve hours.

I can still smell the rubber tires. They would come to a screeching halt, these guys, and in the summer time we'd have the windows open and you could smell this rubber burning from the pavement. We came close to having terrible accidents ourselves.

These guys were no help when it came to first aid. They were voyeurs. They would just stand and watch what was going on, so I never could rely on them to do anything but just lift a patient on a stretcher, and then we'd tear back to the hospital with me crouching in the back of this ambulance on my knees, trying to keep the oxygen on the patient. . . .

One day—I can still see it—we'd gone tearing into this neighborhood. My impression was that it was sort of a poverty neighborhood in the city of Rochester. I remember going up these stairs with these two guys behind me. And there's this small room, white walls, and this big double bed that was too big for the room. And here was this woman, sort of curled up, moaning and groaning in the middle of the bed, and it was a bloody mess. And here is this dead fetus that she had produced, on the bed. I can remember just looking briefly at the baby, and realizing that it was hopeless.

My real concern was for this woman. I knew just enough obstetrics to know that she had to produce the placenta, and if she didn't, the bleeding would continue. I had a terrible time trying to get to her in the middle of the bed. I remember struggling. I had to sort of kneel on the bed, and every time I did, the bed sank down so I had a very difficult time working. She was moaning and groaning, which at least meant she was semi-conscious, and me trying to feel for her uterus and not getting any signs of the placenta.

So, I got out my little black bag and took out a bottle of ergotrate, which would make the uterus clamp down. I can remember thinking to myself, "Well, I'm in a heck of a lot of trouble over this woman and this scene. If I don't give her this medicine she might bleed to death, and if I give it to her she'll probably trap her placenta and then we'll have trouble getting the placenta out and I'll get holy heck for giving her ergotrate." I remember being so nervous. In those days the only way to get the top off a capsule of medicine was with a little saw, and my hand was shaking so with the saw that I could hardly get it through. I finally knocked the top off this little glass vial, pulled the medicine up into the syringe and got it into one of her veins. Thinking that I had at least accomplished that, we picked her up and took her in.

Of course I had looked around for the needle or coat hanger, because I'm sure that's what she'd been after. She was totally isolated, you know. I don't remember anybody saying, "She's my daughter," or "She's my girlfriend." Somebody must have called the E.R., but I don't remember anybody saying, "I'll come to the hospital and see how she is." Nobody came. So we took her in, and the worst part was . . . when I got there . . .

We were very lowly interns. I was a slave to the resident above me. There was a terrific hierarchy in those days. I called the obstetrical resident down, and he was furious! He was furious at me and he was furious at her, at this patient we'd brought in. Boy, he dressed her down right in front of people in the emergency room, and got really angry at me about what did I know about this, and of course, I knew nothing about it. He was a big male, Italian, I'm sure Roman Catholic, and this was very much against his religion. He sort of had a temper tantrum in front of her and in front of me, and lashed out at us both and then finally, reluctantly, admitted her.

I remember thinking, that's not fair to me. Of course I would never have verbalized it. It never would have occurred to me to stand up to the OB resident. You just didn't do that sort of thing. I think a lot of us were silent about our innermost thoughts and feelings.

I remember I went to check on her to see how she was, and she was miserable. She had an infection and was on IV's and antibiotics. That was a dark story . . . a dark picture. I remember thinking, you know, how did she get in this position of being so desperate, and was there no help for her? My feeling was that she was abused by our system of health care. I expected all doctors and all nurses to be sympathetic to patients, and here was just the opposite. Today I would never stand for that. I would have marched into the chief of medicine or the chief of administration and said, "This is not right." It never occurred to me in those days.

My first real experience with abortion was my senior year of medical school, 1951, in Syracuse. I was on surgery as a clerk—as low as you can get on the hierarchy in medicine in those days. A physician came up to me, an obstetrician, and asked whether I would scrub on a case with him, which was unusual because usually you just got assigned cases. I said, "Yes, sir." I can remember him saying, "I need to tell you about it. You know, I have a patient late in her second trimester of pregnancy and she has cancer of the breast." It had just been diagnosed. She had had the breast surgery, and of course almost no matter what you do it's a lethal situation for a woman, because when a woman is pregnant and has cancer of the breast, the cancer just goes hogwild. But he was desperately trying to save this woman's life, and certainly her only hope was to stop the pregnancy by abortion. He could not get the nurses on the surgical floor to scrub, because they would not be part of an abortion. There was not another medical student or resident who would scrub. I never hesitated. I said, "Absolutely." It was never a question. We had an anesthetist, and I remember he and I did all the stuff that the nursing professionals would usually do. I remember saying to myself, "This is not a pleasant thing to witness or be a part of, but my God, we have to save this woman's life!"

She was a young woman, probably in her early thirties. Really sad. I had nothing but respect for this doctor; he was entirely right.

THE ACTIVISTS

The policy of "Confrontation Politics" proved the decisive factor in building the movement. The first radicals who established referral services and laid down the philosophy of complete repeal of abortion laws—Pat Maginnis in San Francisco, William Baird of the Parents Aid society on Long Island and myself—jolted and shocked the public into understanding the issues. It was a crude, inflammatory approach, but the only way to shake the country.

—Lawrence Lader,
Abortion II

Patricia Theresa Maginnis

Patricia Maginnis's name became synonymous with the abortion rights movement in the early 1960s. She was one of the founding members of the National Abortion Rights Action League, which met for the first time in Chicago in 1969. Fiery and witty, she is a passionate advocate of women's rights who sees reproductive issues in a global context. To her, the protection of abortion rights is inseparable from the protection of human rights and the conservation of our planet's resources.

Struggling against her own oppressive Catholic upbringing, she made it her full-time work, for fifteen hard years, to fight against the "institutionalized oppression and inevitable victimization" of women which she sees as inherent in the restriction of abortion rights.

Throughout our conversation she credited other activists who had the courage to take risks along with her and insisted that their contributions be mentioned in the book. She reveals her modesty and the courage to live her beliefs in the story she tells.

I started working on social reform in 1960, and I felt that if I did nothing else in my life, ever, this was something I absolutely had to work on. I had to concentrate on this problem, to the exclusion of all else.

I was brought up in the Catholic Church, where the rule for women is that they are incubators. I felt such an assault on my own personal rights as a human being. To be categorized by ironclad, written-in-stone law that says my uterus is going to dominate me was absolutely unthinkable. I had a very strong base for being totally opposed to the value system of the Catholic Church.

They say that people who leave the Church have a lot of guilt, but instead I had my rages to deal with. I was infuriated at the insulting nature of that system of oppression. I just get furious at any of these religions that demand you give over your health and well-being, your civil rights. I believe that Catholicism is a fundamentalist religion, and that powerful fundamentalist religions dictate what really goes on in the United States.

During my intense concentration on the abortion rights movement, I had very little contact with my family because my mother felt I was totally evil. My brothers and sisters have been gracious—even receptive—to my perspective on the abortion issue, but my mother is still very much a fanatic. Today, at ninety-two, she still rails and harps. Her attitude is: "It's my way, the Church way. All the little eggs must find their partners in life." There are two states that have written into their laws that fertilized eggs are now considered human beings. Arkansas, where my mother lives, is one of them, and I'll just bet you she had a lot to do with it.

I started to get some insight into the importance of reproductive freedom when I was in the Army. In 1952 I was in the Canal Zone in Panama, working in the women's ward as an aide. They brought in a Colombian woman who was married to a Puerto Rican GI. While he was in Korea she had gone to Colombia to visit and had gotten pregnant, and that woman was so distraught over being pregnant that she was a psychiatric case. She couldn't speak English, and nobody there could speak to her in Spanish. They put a cage over the bed and surrounding it, like a storm fence. It was horrible, just horrible. Had our system been different . . . There was nothing for that woman. No counseling, nothing. The nurses would go in there and say, "Shut up." It was so pathetic. She kept crying, "I want eneema, I want eneema." I was twenty-two, still Catholic, but I prayed that poor woman would abort.

Later on there were other things that sent me into a fury. In 1964 I worked for an obstetrician in San Francisco, and I went to an Ob-Gyn meeting where a police official instructed the doctors on what to do if they identified a case of illegal abortion: "We want you doctors to report all these girls as soon as they come into the hospital, before they have support of friends or family. We like to talk to them when they feel their worst." It was just one insult after another.

If you could have seen the form a woman had to fill out if she "claimed" rape! If she "claimed" rape or "claimed" incest, she was dragged in the gutter by what she had to do. And at the end of the form there was a very threatening statement saying something like, "Anyone guilty of perjury is liable to up to six months' imprisonment." That form was in effect until we were able to expose it.

As you may have heard, the word "abortion" was not used by the mass media until 1962. It was always "illegal operation." You see, semantics is so critical in the application of social norms. Words and the way they are put together spell out the way we will be treated. The words "legalized abortion" are anathema. We don't have "legalized tooth extractions" or "legalized vasectomies." The only medical-surgical procedure that carries a stigma is abortion. All other medical-surgical procedures are protected by existing laws, and if they were applied evenly and equally, I'd wager to say that we wouldn't need specific laws concerning abortion. So, we have this thing called "legalized abortion," and that gives those people out there another reason to insist that it be illegalized, demeaned and discredited by using semantic tricks. Women must be absolutely on top of such tricks at all times, because the intention to send us right back to the underground is never said that way. They say they just want to save all these tiny little babies that aren't even born yet.

In 1960, I had the idea that the way to reach the woman in the street was through an opinion poll, so I put together four very naive questions asking people how they felt about abortion and reproduction, and I approached people one by one to get them to talk about this. My friend Robert Bick helped me revise the poll. He is not to be forgotten. He did yeoman's work. We traded fifty dollars and a complete set of Lenin—not linen—for a mimeograph machine. So we had an A.B. Dick, and we rewrote that poll until it asked for a great deal of information. I still have those polls that we got back from doctors and lawyers. It was a way of allowing people to have a say without being frightened of the word "abortion." We went to all legislative hearings, both state and federal, and we let the powers that be know that people weren't afraid of saying the word "abortion."

One day in 1964, when I was living in San Francisco, I received a telegram—I think it was from Lloyd Morrain, who didn't have my telephone number, but he wanted me to know about a lecture at UC Berkeley that evening. It was presented by Garrett Hardin, a geneticist, a prolific author and an excellent thinker. It was very well received, and afterward Frank Lundgren suggested that the lecture be printed up so that we could distribute it. It was an excellent piece of literature, a classic, called "Abortion and Human Dignity." We took out a little ad in the New Republic so people could send for copies of the lecture. After that ad had run for three or four years, we got a letter from the New Republic saying they could no longer publish it. I was absolutely aghast. They felt the ad might be construed as soliciting women to have abortions.

Well, I solicited abortions openly myself, when Rowena Gurner and I put together classes in abortion. We were challenging the California laws which made it a felony to provide information about abortion, and it was important that we do a satisfactory felony so that we could get somewhere, so we handed out leaflets in the street, and we would notify the police in advance about the location of our activity.

Now, I want to tell you an anecdote about Los Gatos, a sleepy little town down near San Jose. Rowena wrote to the police department sending the curriculum of the class, and asked if they would like to send a police officer, and if they did, would they please send a policewoman. Of course, we expected to be arrested, but instead they wrote back and said they did not have the funding to send someone out there, but if we were willing to pay three dollars an hour, they could send a policewoman. (Chuckle.) We always had plainclothes people in attendance. They just loved to come to class, but they never arrested us. A columnist named George Duscheck wrote a column in the *Sunday Examiner* entitled "The Alice in Wonderland of Abortion." It was the funniest column about how in nine counties in California the police would not move against us—these women who were committing the very respectable felonies of soliciting abortion, and helping other women to get abortions. I would have thought this very embarrassing to the police, but they would not arrest us because they did not want those laws challenged. In the business and professions code in California it was a felony to write or talk or give any information about any means or method for inducing abortion. That was the law, and that applied to medical schools, public health departments, everyone. You could not talk about abortion or contraception. Rowena and I were challenging those laws. Eventually we were arrested and remained under felony indictment until 1973 when the Supreme Court stepped in.

The women who gave their all, Lana Phelan and Rowena Gurner, were very much on the scene at that time. Lana was self-educated, very bright and very articulate, a public speaker who could turn a phrase—oh, boy! She had to leave school during the Depression, when she was about fourteen, and she had her first baby when she was fifteen. Lana worked in the city attorney's office, and she got word from her boss that if she spoke about abortion she would be fired, but she didn't back down, and she lost her job. Rowena Gurner had a lot of foresight, a lot of savvy. She had a good business mind, and she was quite creative. These were some of the people who put together the movement. We were working sixty hours a week, with no pay. I worked a part-time job as a medical technologist, and I was able at that time to sell a pint of blood from time to time, because I have a fairly rare type.

When we put together the class on abortion, we drew up a leaflet. Rowena would send me off with stacks of these to give out on the street. The leaflet outlined the four sections of the class. The first part of the class was about the law, the second part was about contraception, thanks to Rowena—that was her thing. The third part was about Mexico and Puerto Rico: how to get your abortion through the underground, including a list of available abortionists; and the fourth part was about self-induced abortion by what Rowena called the digital method. We ran from one to three classes a week. The phone never stopped ringing from morning till night. People in terrible distress, frantic. Once people came to the class, we made them do certain things to help us, such as writing three letters to their legislators. They could say anything they wanted, but they had to sign the letter with a name and an address.

We ran the classes from 1966 until about 1969, mostly in California, but we also went to Portland, Washington, D.C., Cleveland, Albuquerque. While we were in Washington, D.C., doing our class, a little old woman came hobbling up to me on her cane. She took me aside and she said, "Don't tell anyone my secret. My mother died from an abortion. We were little girls then. My father walked us eight miles through the snow and ice to the hospital to see my mother, and she looked like she was asleep, and I said, 'Mommy, are you going to finish our First Communion dresses?' and my father was crying." To help her abort, someone had put kerosene in her uterus. Here was this poor woman at the age of eighty-four saying, "Don't tell anyone my secret."

We decided that the whole enormous set of dangers for women had to be exposed. We needed to bring the underground overground. We could put together a list of names and phone numbers of people women could contact in Mexico,

Puerto Rico, and Japan, but there were all sorts of complications that women didn't realize they might have to deal with. We wanted to give women a whole education about the underground. Terrible things could happen. For instance, although we tried desperately to prevent it, unscrupulous people would get hold of that list of abortionists and sell it for three hundred dollars!

Women had to be educated, because the naive woman looking for Dr. Paris in Tijuana might end up with somebody else. Most of the women didn't speak Spanish and didn't know what to do. Dr. Paris could have decided to take the day off, and just farmed out his practice to somebody else. If the woman was lucky, it would be somebody who knew what he or she was doing. There was no extradition for cases of illegal abortion, so the doctors couldn't be prosecuted in this country, no matter what they did to you. Of course, abortion was illegal in Mexico, too, but the Mexican police were paid off.

When we relegate abortion to the underworld we are putting dangerous tools in the hands of naive people or greedy people.

When we were sending people to Mexico for abortions, we had three reports of doctors who raped the women they were treating. We found out that one doctor had raped two women in the same day. When women are at the mercy of a cutthroat system, anything can happen to them. The whole thing was like walking on floating ice.

I really wish that Rowena and Lana could tell you their stories too. The Schlesinger Library at Radcliffe was doing oral histories in 1974 or 1975 of women who were involved in the abortion rights movement. They have transcripts from Lana Phelan, Dr. Lonny Meyers, and Dr. Sadja Goldsmith Greenwood. You should read Lonny Meyers' and Sadja Goldsmith's interviews. They are very touching. Those women were involved very early, and they were there at the founding of NARAL in January of 1969 in Chicago. Larry Lader and I were among the founding members, along with an Episcopal minister. It is interesting that the Schlesinger project chose only women, because Dr. Ben Munson in South Dakota is certainly one of the early pioneers. He was getting in touch with us as early as 1964 or 1965. He was the only doctor providing abortions in five states. Oh, my goodness, what that man went through!

I've pulled out of the movement. I'm struggling with an old house that's getting older, and I'm getting old, and we're getting old together. I haven't been active in the movement since about 1976. I'm grateful for Larry Lader and Bill Baird and Shaw and folks like that who are holding it up, because I just burned out. It was fifteen years at hard labor, and it was twenty-four hours a day. It just didn't go away. It was a pretty dramatic time, but not something that most people would want to be bogged down in for a long time.

My feeling is that we cannot talk about these things enough. Women must be reminded, the citizenry of our world needs to be reminded, that we must have control of our reproductive lives. When you create a situation in which the control over women's bodies and minds is put at the mercy of those in power, then you also institutionalize the misuse of power against them. This is why I say that when the dominating, pious attitudes of the fundamentalist religions become law, they put women, and also children, at risk.

Anti-abortion laws would rebuild the underground, and underground abortion makes women victims in more ways than simply having to scurry around like a pack of rats looking for relief. The fertility of the human species is so enormous that during the female reproductive life there are some four hundred possible pregnancies, and the implications are enormous for our continued existence on earth. Every time a human being comes into the world it puts a strain on the planet. There are thousands of children who die of starvation every year, in spite of Mother Teresa.

There was an article in a San Francisco paper on October 4, 1984, describing practices that took place in the 1800s when there were enormous numbers of homeless orphan children.

These children would be put on trains and sent to other cities where, on a particular day you could simply go down to the train station, meet the train, and get a child. Who knows what happened to those children who were "adopted?"

Look what we've done to countries that are now eager to have family-planning programs with abortion as a backup, which they desperately need. Our pious administration has denied that, resulting in thousands of children dying of starvation. This is what happens to all those unborn eggs striving for personhood that they say they're protecting.

Of course, the connection between power and greed is so close, the point has been made that the aberrant power structure we have now would want to encourage the enormous population explosion which would create a huge underclass—slavery almost. They would not admit that, I'm sure, and it may not even be a conscious thing, but the implications seem to be there.

People are beginning to realize the connection between our dominant egotistical attitudes and the destruction of our environment. Finally, finally, we are beginning to give a voice to concerns about how toxic we humans are. No other species is so destructive, on such an ego trip.

This is not a single issue. Even though the abortion rights question may be dominating the area of social thought, and people who are struggling to protect women's rights may have to be single-minded about the struggle in order to make their point, it is always a part of the greater social, environmental condition.

simply to submit to the Massachusetts court, or to make them extradite me. There were pros and cons. If we made them extradite, then I would have to undergo the experience of being arrested by the Ohio State Police. Undoubtedly, the media would be present and I would be in a scene, getting arrested and handcuffed with the cameras going in the presence of my wife and my two children. And then we'd have to go through extradition, which would take some time and be costly. Those would be the negatives. On the other hand, by going through extradition we would get the issues of the case out in the open in Ohio, in an Ohio court, in relatively neutral territory because the indictment was not an Ohio one. And possibly we could get some good public exposure on the issues and that could potentially be to our benefit.

But then ultimately, we realized that the Governor, who would finally decide whether or not to give me over to Massachusetts, was not in our corner. I'd end up in Massachusetts anyway, with Massachusetts being all the more angry, having spent the time and the effort to get me. So, Gerry got on the phone with the prosecutor in Massachusetts and was able to work a deal. The arrest warrant would be withdrawn on the promise that Gerry would submit me to the court on a given date. So we decided to go that way; simply to submit voluntarily.

Gerry and I flew up to Massachusetts, kept the appointment and wandered into court and I presented myself to the Judge. We hammed it up a little bit I guess [chuckling]. I put on liturgical garb for going to court—this was a form of liturgy—and the poor judge, and the bailiff and the prosecutor and the prosecutor's assistant just didn't know what to do with this. Here I was, standing there in a black suit and a white collar in Cambridge, Massachusetts—a predominantly Catholic territory—answering an indictment on abortion. This was inconceivable.

Anyway, I was arraigned, booked, and released on my own recognizance. They did not put bail on me. I filled out forms and we got on a plane and flew back to Cleveland to get busy

then with the actual legal case. What had happened—the most
amazing thing—was that the grand jury had given the prosecutor a "unit indictment" against the physician, and me, the
minister. The unit is not a common instrument, but it is occa-
sionally used in conspiratorial cases. It permits the grand jury to
indict more than one person as if they were one. Technically, it
means that unless the court subsequently chooses to break the
unit, they are tried and found guilty or innocent as a unit, and
convicted as a unit, and sentenced as a unit. The first order of
business, from the standpoint of my attorneys, was to file a petition for the severance of the unit. From early July onward, we
were back and forth from Cleveland to Massachusetts. I got to
know those airplanes rather well. But we were successful on the
first round, which gave us some hope. The judge who heard the
petition for the severing of the unit agreed that the nature of
the roles played did not justify the unit. The prosecutor had
apparently allowed the grand jury the illusions that I'd have
some larger role, that maybe there'd been some payoff, that I
got a kickback from the physician for having referred a client to
him. I readily admitted to what I'd actually done, and the judge
quickly saw that the unit indictment should be severed. So my
indictment, then, continued as a separate case. One of the ironies of this is that I never met Dr. Brunelle. Our cases got
separated, and he was rather quickly brought to trial, convicted,
and sent to prison. He was in prison by the end of 1969.

My case was very different and became much more con-
voluted. We first filed motions for dismissal of the indictment
against me on a variety of grounds. One was constitutionality.
We argued that the Massachusetts statute under which the indictment was brought was invalid. Jurisdiction was another. We
argued that Massachusetts did not have jurisdiction to bring indictment against me as an Ohio resident, that I'd never been
inside of Massachusetts, that I'd committed no crime in Massachusetts. My behavior was performed in Ohio, not in that state.
Separation of church and state was another: that I was an ordained clergy functioning in my ministerial role of pastoral

counseling. Confidentiality—or what the law calls privileged information—was fourth. The fifth was the facts. We argued that the facts of my behavior did not constitute the crime with which I was charged. I'd been charged with aiding and abetting in the performance of that specific abortion, and I'd been charged with serving as an accessory before the fact. So, we filed motions for dismissal on these various grounds.

Of course, the wheels of justice move slowly: various court appearances for filing motions, and finally dates set for arguing the motion. That did not occur until Monday of Holy Week, 1970, about nine months later. On Monday we were in court all day presenting the arguments for the motions of dismissal and over into Tuesday morning and finally finished up before noon on Tuesday morning and went back to Cleveland to wait for a decision. And on Good Friday we got a decision, which was that the indictment was dismissed. The judge's last name was Roy, Judge Roy. We were delighted and pleased. And so we thought we'd done it. We had a party, a victory party among lots of friends that Saturday night, the night before Easter. Friends had organized the Bob Hare Defense Committee and had been getting out mailings to all kinds of people, enclosing forms for people to use to send us still more names and addresses of interested parties to raise funds for my defense. We got all the defense committee people and lots of friends together at a big celebration Saturday night, and were pleased for this outcome, which we thought was just: Judge Roy had ruled that the facts of my behavior did not, indeed, constitute the crime with which I was charged. He thereby avoided all the tough issues. The constitutionality, and the privileged information, confidentiality, and the church and state. All of those things. We had expected that would be the case, but we were nevertheless disappointed that he did not extend himself to make any rulings on any of the issues. In any case, it was over, I was free, and we were pleased.

Within three weeks we received notice that the prosecutor had established grounds for filing a new appeal against Judge

Roy's dismissal order, and he was taking the case to the appellate level. It wasn't over and now we were going to have to fight the case at the Massachusetts Supreme Judicial Court.

On technical grounds the prosecutor argued that Judge Roy erred in the issuance of the dismissal order . . . it meant that we had to prepare to present the arguments at the Supreme Judicial Court. Again, it took months to get into the Appellate Court and we had a long hiatus where nothing was happening. During this time, I continued my work in Cleveland to develop the free-floating congregation. I did not continue my participation in the Clergy Consultation Services while the case was pending—but other people continued.

As a means of fund-raising, my Ohio attorney and I went out and did public speaking. The cause became a cause célèbre. People heard about it—church groups and other groups, and I would get invitations to speak. And from those groups and those speaking occasions would often come significant financial contributions to support the defense of the case.

Throughout the case we did get a lot of church support— particularly from my own denomination, the Presbyterians, and from the Episcopal Church. We got the Episcopal bishop in Cleveland to be the co-chair of my defense committee along with my presbytery executive. That is the term we happen to use, the presbytery—or regional unit of the Church. Once we become ordained, we clergy are members of the presbytery. While it's a collective, democratic body, nevertheless it has ecclesiastical jurisdiction for its clergy members.

The presbytery did investigate the question of my ordination status in relationship to my being criminally indicted. That was an ecclesiastical process. There were fellow clergy in my presbytery—the Presbytery of Cleveland—who really were quite up in arms. They took the position that I was operating in violation of my ordination vows, let alone in violation of the civil law, and that this was grounds for my being defrocked. So the Presbytery instituted an investigatory committee to study the question of my ordination standing. That turned out very positively also.

The committee recommended no further action and illuminated the position that my engagement in this kind of counseling was very much within the bounds of ordination vows. When that report came to a vote in the Presbytery about 25 percent voted against it and 75 percent for it. Those were not bad odds: 3 to 1. My neck was saved ecclesiastically and I was not removed from the ordained ministry.

It was another eighteen months, into late '71 before we finally got to the Supreme Judicial Court of Massachusetts. Irony of ironies, the court docket on which I was scheduled also had Teddy Kennedy, who had an appeal on his Chappaquiddick incident. I still have the court docket with my name and Teddy Kennedy's right across from each other. We got before the Supreme Court, the motions were argued, and my attorneys felt that the prosecutor had been foolish to proceed, and probably did not stand a respectable chance of winning his appeal. But nevertheless we had to go through with it. It was March of '72 when we finally got the opinion from the Supreme Judicial Court. To our utter astonishment they had ruled in his favor, in a peculiar way, however. Typically, when appellate courts rule, they simply render their opinion in a quick memorandum, and that's it. In this case they attached an advisory memorandum in which they essentially said, "We find your arguments, Mr. Prosecutor, valid on the technical grounds and therefore have to answer your appeal in the affirmative. However, the facts of Reverend Hare's behavior do not seem to us to warrant any further prosecution." It was not customary for them to offer such an opinion, but they offered it anyway: "Here's your appeal, but why don't you quit." He would not. So in March of 1972, the indictment was reinstated, and we had to start all over again to see if we could find some other avenues by which to quash the thing.

The process from March of '72 was slow and tedious. My attorneys found some additional grounds on which to file motions for dismissal. And the case dragged through 1972. As you know, on January 22, 1973, the Federal Supreme Court struck down all the abortion statutes with its *Roe* v. *Wade* decision, so my case fell and the prosecutor had nothing more he could do and we were at last free and clear.

My attorneys had not been billing us regularly for those last months. Finally, Gerry said, "Whatever's in the defense fund— split it between us and call it quits." They should have, in the end, received considerably more than they did. All those funds had been raised by the Bob Hare Defense Committee, and it never cost me a single penny.

That's the story of the case, the way I fell into it, and the way it proceeded.

I thought the Supreme Court decision of '73 was correct. I received it with relief, knowing that now doctors and women could be about the business of women's health care and fertility and reproduction without being under threat of prosecution.

My sense of things politically, theologically, and ecclesiastically is that we're in a very tough time and I don't see that it's going to get any easier. The battle to preserve *Roe* v. *Wade* is going to be a hard battle. I wish that weren't the case, but I think that's going to be the case. It would be a disaster if it were overturned.

A VOICE FROM
THE DARKNESS

Anonymous

During the years when abortion was illegal, any one of us who participated in an abortion in any way committed a crime. Those of us who lived through those years know how many ordinary, law-abiding people like ourselves were considered criminals. And since so many of us were intimately affected by the illegality of abortion, we were all forced into public and private silence. None of us wanted to be known as criminals or social deviants.

Women who were able to find their way to an abortionist seem to feel they were the lucky ones. Sometimes an abortionist surfaced close to home, but often women traveled out of state or out of the country, as much to protect their anonymity as to find the abortion. Fear of exposure led women to risk their lives meeting with dubious strangers in abandoned buildings, twenty-five-watt-bulb hotels, and empty parking lots. Frightened and alone, they knocked on doors in the sleaziest parts of town, spoke in cryptic codes, and used passwords. They counted out hundreds of dollars in small bills, spent their salaries, all their savings and borrowed money. They skulked like outlaws in the shadows of community censure, made criminals by legislation.

Even the sexual revolution offered little relief. Women began to talk with each other about their fears and to tap into an underground; information about abortion became a bit more accessible, but nothing really changed. It was still a crime in all the same ways.

The following article was published in Cavalier *magazine in 1969. The author pleads for an end to the social pressure which forced her to conceal her real name. Those years are thankfully behind us. We are no longer silenced by the fear of prosecution. As the mythology surrounding procreation and sexual behavior fades, we are beginning to talk about the past openly. The stories in this book could not have been written during those fearful years when abortion was legally unavailable. Only now can we look back, from the safe and distant present, and see ourselves as prey.*

"Dr. Spencer Is Just Down the Street"*

I didn't read Dr. Spencer's obit over the breakfast table, as did untold thousands of his other ex-patients. My husband brings the newspaper home from the university, so I'm always several hours behind the rest of America. When he pointed out the item, I let out an involuntary, "Oh, no!"

"Why are you so sad, Mommy!" asked my five-year-old.

"Because a good man died," I answered. "A very good man indeed."

"Was he old?"

I nodded, feeling teary and uncomposed.

"Then you shouldn't be sad. Just like you told me with Grandma, old people die when their lives end. Right?"

"Yes, honey, that's true. But he was a very special man. I'll tell you about him someday."

I thought of all the bowed heads out there that day. Maybe even some rosary masses and some sitting of Shivahs. And I thought about the middle-aged, middle-class ladies of my generation who read the same obit and who made appropriately liberal comments about how interesting it was that one man had

---

*Originally published in *Cavalier* magazine, 1969.

performed so many abortions and how necessary it is to liberalize the abortion laws, whereupon their middle-aged, middle-class husbands nodded assent, never for a second dreaming that their very own wives might have journeyed to Ashland, Pennsylvania, in the days of their defiant youth.

But, unlike too many of my peers who choose to forget, I remember what it was like for those of us of the pre-pill diaphragm generation during the early fifties. Dr. Spencer was our guru.

We made love, those of us who identified with Kerouac and Ginsberg (little did we know that they were not interested), who patronized art movies (the summer festival at the Thalia in New York was big time), who hated Joe McCarthy, who loved James Agee, who dug sounds of Charlie Parker and Billie Holliday. We learned in our anthropology courses about cultural relativism and in our literature courses about those seventeenth-century swingers, and we added it up as an ode to sexual freedom. Freedom also to leave our Margaret Sanger diaphragms around in bureau drawers so that our fathers would spend the whole night throwing up and questioning what went wrong.

In a *Realist* interview, Dr. Spencer talked about the poor souls who came to him after having been raped by psychiatrists, D.A.s, and even priests. It wasn't like that for us—no rapes, no incest, no fears of German measles maiming our unborn children. Our generation was called "Silent" and "Beat," but some of us did manage to express ourselves in bed.

Dr. Spencer didn't ask personal questions, and he didn't moralize. He was just there, out there in Ashland, like Mecca and Jerusalem and Lourdes and all of the other shrines to which people are drawn in times of need.

I visited Ashland several times between 1953 and 1955, once for my own pregnancy and later as an accompanist for friends. Dr. Spencer always specified on the telephone that the patient bring a girl friend. I never asked him the reason, but I suspect he thought that the presence of men, especially in the hotel, might rile the townspeople. He was probably right.

Sleepy-eyed and dreary—that describes Ashland. Four or five thousand people (*The New York Times* said twelve thousand, but I don't believe it) housed in winding tiers above the main street. The heyday of coal mining was over; and despite what people might have said publicly about Dr. Spencer (it's always fashionable to condemn crime), he was obviously good business for the town. At a gas station, we were told, without asking, "Dr. Spencer is just down the street." The druggist said cheerfully, "I suppose you want the Sunday *Times*. I always get a pile of 'em for you girls," and the hotel clerk commented matter-of-factly, "You'll just be here for tonight." No question mark.

My first trip, my *own* trip, took place on Easter weekend. Dr. Spencer was a pathologist, a general practitioner, and a specialist in chest diseases. And even on a Saturday afternoon— which must have been his busiest day for the working girls and students and, yes, mothers (a frail, very young girl, a mother of four, told me that she had wanted to come during the week to "avoid the crowd" but that her husband couldn't get off work to babysit)—the waiting room of his eleven-room clinic was lined with several "legitimate" patients. On the walls there were displayed the usual diplomas (his medical degree was from the University of Pennsylvania in 1916), plus several eerie hair wreaths, those framed Victorian ornaments containing bits of hair from now-deceased relatives. But on the operating walls and on those of the numerous recovery rooms (each of which had a bed as well as a chair for the faithful companion) were hundreds, maybe thousands, of small wooden plaques from souvenir shops painted with homespun philosophy and witticisms, all diabolically appropriate. As I emerged from anesthesia, I saw one that read, "Today Is the Tomorrow You Dreaded So Much Yesterday." Another one that etched itself in my memory was, "If You're Out Driving, Don't Park. That's How Accidents Happen."

My initial interview with Dr. Spencer couldn't have been more relaxing or more reassuring. He was small, almost frail, with wispy white hair; I thought he was at least eighty then and was startled to learn that he died at seventy-nine, some sixteen years later. After asking a couple of questions to establish the onset of pregnancy, he began a soft-spoken but passionate diatribe about the need for better abortion laws. He spoke of Thomas Paine and Charles Darwin and especially of Abraham Lincoln, who, he said, "consciously broke bad laws." Then, after producing from the bowels of his cluttered desk a hand-printed document, protected by torn cellophane—which outlined his philosophy and his justification for his "crime," he asked me to sign a strangely worded and obviously meaningless paper, agreeing to assume half of the court costs in case of his arrest. When I returned with a friend a few months later, he had abandoned that part of the ritual, muttering, "My files were getting too full anyway."

The injection that he gave me on that afternoon was something he called his own secret. "I can't tell you what's in it, but I promise it won't hurt, and it'll start things up just enough so I can finish tomorrow morning."

I spent the evening watching a dreadful double bill at the local movie house (I remember distinctly having suffered through Hopalong Cassidy, but it couldn't have been, not in 1953), slept well, and arrived at his office the next morning just as the church bells were tolling the joys of Easter. My friend reported that, as he was about to begin the curettage (a process that took, from the time he administered the sodium pentothal [an anesthetic] until I woke up, about half an hour), a farmer appeared at the operating room door and asked him to go fishing. "Nope, I've got a busy day. Gotta get these girls started home before the heavy traffic," he replied.

Later, as I lay serenely in the comfort of the white-sheeted bed, the church bells were still ringing and I was convinced that the man that Christianity was heralding that day was Dr. Spencer. I could not have felt more exultation than I did as Dr. Spencer patted my hand. "Diaphragms don't work in the medicine chest," he said, after establishing the fact that I owned one, "and I don't like to see any patient more than once."

He presented me with a pile of envelopes, each containing enough medication to supply several post-abortion patients.

One was labeled ambiguously "T.P.M." "That one means 'to prevent milk,'" he chuckled. "I don't want any nosey mothers to get upset."

When I paid him the forty dollars, I kissed his cheek. And note well: no mention of payment was made until after the operation. I heard that he willingly skipped the fee for hardship cases; even when he was involved in court cases, he never charged more than one hundred dollars.

"Go get yourself a good meal at the hotel before you start back," he advised. "You'll probably see a few of the other girls there too, but listen, don't act like you recognize them, okay?"

So there we were, eating a traditional ham and sweet potatoes Easter dinner in a daffodil-decorated dining room, empty except for four other Spencer "couples." What a fitting close to the only meaningful Easter of my life—it was I who had risen and I who had been given a new life. I wanted to sing and dance.

I telephoned my parents en route back to campus, pretending, of course, that I'd spent a quiet day in the library; and when my mother asked timidly (she was accustomed to angry denunciation of all those holidays to which I'd been subjected as a child) if I'd had "anything special to eat," I gleefully described the entire menu, beginning with the daffodils and ending with the lemon pie. I think I might have even thrown in something about the jubilant sound of the bells. It was a good Easter for her, too.

For the next few years, I was besieged with requests for particulars about Dr. Spencer. For reasons unclear to me, many of his patients were reluctant to pass on information. I became known as "the source," and I was approached by nervous boys and swollen-eyed girls, all of whom talked about their "friend in trouble." Once there was a midnight call from the West Coast. The caller refused to say how she had been told about me, but I was a pushover for anyone's "friend in trouble." To withhold information about the Saint of Ashland was, to me, equivalent to being an accessory to a crime, for I, too, believed that bad laws should be broken. Maybe I saw myself as Mrs. Lincoln or

Mrs. Paine—who knows? In any case, I was proud to steer the needy toward Ashland.

The experiences of those who visited other abortionists were grim indeed. One girl, in the clutches of a demented old lady wielding a germ-infested catheter ("I insert it, dearie, and to-morrow you have a few pains, that's all") was forced to describe in detail the extent of her "sin." She spent three weeks in the hospital with a serious infection that rendered her permanently sterile.

Then there was my friend whose boyfriend's parents were footing the abortion bill. They wouldn't allow her to go to Dr. Spencer, feeling, in the great tradition of those who believe "you get what you pay for," that forty dollars wasn't enough to guarantee a competent job. She was met in a hotel room by two men who stuffed a towel into her mouth so she wouldn't yell. No anesthesia, of course, because, "We want you to remember this and not mess around anymore." She passed out at one point, and they dutifully waited until she revived before con-tinuing the massacre, while, at the same time, the boyfriend's parents were bragging to their suburban friends how they'd paid eight hundred dollars for "two of the best doctors in New York."

So, those of us who had experienced the warmth and kind-ness of Dr. Spencer were doubly grateful. I couldn't bring my-self to buy any of those corny plaques for him, but I had friends who did; and I remember one girl who sent him a hand-woven smoking jacket. A sentimental thank-you note and a birth an-nouncement when my first child was born were all I ever man-aged. I sometimes speculated if he recognized my name when it cropped up so often as a "referral."

During my early years as a faculty wife, I suggested Dr. Spencer to a few students. It was often difficult to contact him because he kept trying to retire. At that time he sent out mim-eographed instructions on contacting other doctors in Cuba—until Castro denounced both prostitution and abortion as equiv-alent vices—and in Puerto Rico. (Several years ago, *The Realist* solicited contributions for an around-the-world trip for him and his wife, which they took.) And in recent years, nothing—but then, students with whom I'm in contact now have a whole different bag.

Dr. Spencer's coterie spoke of him as mad and crazy and eccentric, and we meant these labels as adulatory. He once asked two friends, one white and one black, if they were sisters. They laughed, undoubtedly with some embarrassment, and he said, as he looked at them for the first time, "Oh, golly, excuse me. But you know, Lincoln wouldn't have noticed either."

He was wrong, of course, about Lincoln. Dr. Spencer misunderstood a lot of history. When I heard that he sported a Goldwater button before the 1962 election, I was stunned. Then I realized that it figured—that is, it figured for him. The individual rebel, the individual act, the individual protest—all of this he identified correctly with the best of the conservatives but wrongly with the current batch for whom their emasculated creed is thinly masked bigotry and cold-warrior aggressiveness. Dr. Spencer was a conservative who was an ardent atheist, a conservative who disapproved of gun registration, a conservative who won the support of the United Mine Workers Union because of his willingness to go down into the mines to aid injured miners, a conservative who maintained that outlawing premarital sex wouldn't work any better than Prohibition. You see, it figures.

When I left Ashland, I felt cleansed, grateful, and free, and my experience was repeated many thousand times. In destroying a life (and I never deceived myself about that: I wept bitterly a few weeks later when I found in a biology book a life-size drawing of an eight-week embryo), he saved mine. He saved me from a life with a man I didn't love, and he freed me for the life I have now with a superb husband and two magnificent daughters.

When this—what should I call it: testimonial? eulogy? chronicle?—is published, I'll save it to show my daughters, hoping that by the time they read it, they'll be appalled at my having published it anonymously, but that they'll understand enough about me to forgive the cowardice of a mother for whom the world is not all that she wants it to be.

BIBLIOGRAPHY

American Friends Service Committe, *Who Shall Live? Man's Control Over Birth and Death*, New York, Hill and Wang, 1970.

Devereux, George, *A Study of Abortion in Primitive Societies*, New York, Julian Press, 1955.

Felman, David M., *Marital Relations, Birth Control, and Abortion in Jewish Law*, New York, Shocken Books, 1966.

Gordon, Linda, *Women's Body, Woman's Right: A Social History of Birth Control in America*, New York, Grossman, 1976.

Hall, Robert E. M.D., ed., *Abortion in a Changing World: Proceedings of an International Conference Convened in Hot Springs, Virginia, November 17–20, 1968, by the Association for the Study of Abortion*, vol. 1, New York Columbia University Press, 1970.

Lader, Lawrence, *Abortion*, Indianapolis, Bobbs-Merrill, 1966.

———, *Abortion II: Making the Revolution*, Boston, Beacon Press, 1973.

Mohr, James C., *Abortion in America: The Origin and Evolution of National Policy, 1800–1900*, New York, Oxford University Press, 1978.

Rosen, Harold, ed., *Therapeutic Abortion*, New York, Julian Press, 1954.